Our selection of the city's best places to
eat, drink and experience:

◉ Sights

✖ Eating

☕ Drinking

✪ Entertainment

🔒 Shopping

These symbols give you the vital
information for each listing:

- ✆ Telephone Numbers
- ⊘ Opening Hours
- P Parking
- @ Internet Access
- 🛜 Wi-Fi Access
- ✔ Vegetarian Selection
- 🗌 English-Language Menu
- ✪ Family-Friendly
- 🚌 Bus
- ⛴ Ferry
- Ⓜ Metro
- Ⓢ Subway
- 🚋 Tram
- 🚆 Train

Find each listing quickly on maps
for each neighbourhood:

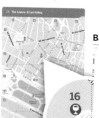

Bar Hemingway

Lonely Planet's
Singapore

Lonely Planet Pocket Guides
are designed to get you
straight to the heart of the city.

Inside you'll find all the
must-see sights, plus tips to
make your visit to each one
really memorable. We've split
the city into easy-to-navigate
neighbourhoods and provided
clear maps so you'll find your
way around with ease. Our
expert authors have searched
out the best of the city: walks,
food, nightlife and shopping,
to name a few. Because you
want to explore, our 'Local Life'
pages will take you to some
of the most exciting areas to
experience the real Singapore.

And of course you'll find all
the practical tips you need for
a smooth trip: itineraries for
short visits, how to get around,
and how much to tip the guy
who serves you a drink at the
end of a long day's exploration.

It's your guarantee of a
really great experience.

Our Promise

QuickStart Guide 7

Explore Singapore 21

Worth a Trip:

The Best of Singapore 151

Singapore's Best Walks

Singapore's Best ...

Survival Guide 175

QuickStart Guide

Welcome to Singapore

Smart, sharp and just a little sexy, Singapore is Southeast Asia's new 'It kid', subverting staid old stereotypes with ambitious architecture, dynamic museums, celebrity chefs and hip boutiques. Spike it all with smoky temples, gut-rumble-inducing food markets and pockets of steamy jungle, and you too might find that Asia's 'wallflower' is a much more intriguing bloom than you ever gave it credit for.

Merlion, designed by Fraser Brunner, Merlion Park, Marina Bay (Map p30)
RICHARD L'ANSON/LONELY PLANET IMAGES ©

Singapore
Top Sights

Singapore Zoo (p134)

Singapore Zoo is one of the world's most inviting, enlightened animal sanctuaries, and a family-friendly must. Breakfast with orang-utans, sail on a jungle-fringed reservoir and purr over rare white tigers.

Singapore Botanic Gardens (p122)

Singapore's Garden of Eden is the perfect antidote to the city's rat-race tendencies. Obscenely lush and verdant, its 63 hectares are home to rare orchids, a swan-studded lake and a romantic French restaurant.

Night Safari (p136)

Get up close and personal with a different kind of nightlife at this award-winning wildlife park, filled with an intriguing cast of free-roaming and free-flying creatures, great and small.

National Museum of Singapore (p24)

Evocative, interactive exhibitions and striking old-meets-new architecture define Singapore's showcase museum. If you're after a gripping crash course in Singaporean history and culture, put this on your hit list.

Asian Civilisations Museum (p26)

Travel east to west across Asia at this engrossing ode to the continent's tapestry of cultures and traditions. It's like a glittering cultural attic, filled with ancient pottery and sculptures, mystical weaponry and precious jewels.

Universal Studios (p112)

Home to the planet's tallest duelling roller coasters, Universal Studios cranks up the adrenalin with seven themed areas pimped with enough rides, razzle-dazzle spectaculars and movie-set kitsch to thrill the most hardened of inner children.

LIAO	MÀ	SHĪ	XIĀN	ZHĔN	LIÁN
林	梅	苏	谢	甄	林
LÍN	MÉI	SŪ	XIÈ	ZHĒN	LÍN
刘	莫	谭	杨	朱	卢
LIÚ	MÒ	TÁN	YÁNG	ZHŪ	LÚ
卢	彭	唐	叶	庄	陆
LÚ	PÉNG	TÁNG	YÈ	ZHUĀNG	LÙ
陆	邱	吴	余	胡	罗

Chinatown Heritage Centre (p64)

Immerse yourself in the struggles, scandals and hard-core grit of Chinatown's roller-coaster past at this unsung museum. You'll find it on a lantern-festooned street once better known for opium dens and coolie traders.

Raffles Hotel (p28)

Yes, it's a cliché, but legend permeates this hotel's whitewashed walls like no other. Channel the days of the British Empire in its tropical gardens or sip like Somerset Maugham in the atmospheric Bar & Billiard Room.

Southern Ridges (p140)

Monkey-peppered jungle, sculptural forest walkways, and sunset cocktails overlooking the South China Sea – this multipark trail offers one of Singapore's most beautiful and accessible natural getaways. (Henderson Waves, p141)

Singapore
Local Life

Insider tips to help you find the real city

Once you've checked off the major sights, dig a little deeper and discover a more intimate side to the city – the side the locals know.

Chinatown Tastebuds & Temples (p66)

▶ Authentic hawker centres
▶ Hip bars and restaurants

The opium dens may have gone, but Chinatown's stubborn spirit kicks on in its in-yer-face market stalls, congee-slurping uncles and dragon-littered temples. Whether plonked on a plastic *kopitiam* (coffee-shop) stool or offering incense to the divine, prepare to savour enticing Chinatown.

Tiong Bahru (p82)

▶ Hip shops, bars and cafes
▶ Heritage architecture

Not only famous for its art deco and mid-20th-century domestic architecture, this low-rise,

laid-back neighbourhood is pulling in the trend-setters and hipsters with its ever-expanding booty of clued-in cafes, trendy bars and restaurants, and quirky shops, not to mention its top-notch bookstore.

A Stroll in Little India (p86)

▶ Mosques and temples
▶ Street life

A riot of colours, scents and evening crowds, Little India bursts with pungent pavement stalls, authentic Indian grub and sari-peddling shops blaring Indian pop. Hunt down market spices, pimp your skin with henna, and feast your eyes on a whimsical, fairy-tale mosque.

Katong (p104)

▶ Peranakan heritage
▶ Restaurants

Multicoloured heritage shophouses, restaurant-filled streets and shops peddling traditional ceramics, shoes and textiles – popular Katong is the heart and soul of Singapore's Peranakan culture. At its southern end is cycle-friendly East Coast Park, dotted with seafood restaurants and bars facing a boat-laden sea.

Geylang (p106)

▶ Nightlife
▶ Street food

Gateway between heaven and hell, Geylang is as famed for its temples and mosques as it is for its *lorong* (alley) brothels, girly bars and cheap

SIMON RICHMOND/LONELY PLANET IMAGES ©

Tiong Bahru

Buddha Tooth Relic Temple & Museum, Chinatown (p70)

ANDERS BLOMQVIST/LONELY PLANET IMAGES ©

hotel rooms. Slip in at night for brilliant street food, karaoke and a rush that's more 'cheeky Bangkok' than 'strait-laced Singapore'.

Changi & Pulau Ubin (p108)

▶ Changi Prison Museum & Chapel
▶ Quaint villages

Laid-back Changi peddles batik fabrics, Indian textiles, and harrowing stories of Singapore under Japanese occupation at the moving Changi Prison Museum & Chapel. Further afield, bicycle-friendly Pulau Ubin island channels a long-forgotten Singapore of ramshackle villages, jungle, old plantations and quiet country lanes.

Other great places to experience the city like a local:

Yet Con (p38)

Public Bus 14 (p35)

One Price Store (p58)

Tanjong Pagar Distripark (p73)

Golden Mile Complex (p97)

Kerbau Rd Beer Garden (p98)

Haji Lane (p102)

Nrityalaya Aesthetics Society (p101)

Singapore Turf Club (p127)

Sri Muneeswaran Hindu Temple (p132)

Singapore
Day Planner

Day One

Start your Singapore fling with a local breakfast of *kaya* (coconut jam)toast, runny eggs and strong *kopi* (coffee) at **Ya Kun Kaya Toast** (p74) before a riverside stroll at the **Quays** (p22) for a jaw-dropping panorama of brazen skyscrapers and refined colonial buildings. Dive into the brilliant **Asian Civilisations Museum** (p26) or keep walking to the **National Museum of Singapore** (p24) or the **Peranakan Museum** (p32) for some cultural insight, then fill up on Singapore's best chilli crab at riverside **Jumbo Seafood** (p37).

Fingers licked, head to nearby Chinatown to feast your eyes on the technicolor **Sri Mariamman Temple** (p70) and the epic **Buddha Tooth Relic Temple** (p70). Check out the kitsch souvenirs on and around Temple St, then give your feet some reflexology lovin' at **People's Park Complex** (p79).

Recharged, sip a cheeky cocktail at rooftop **La Terraza** (p76) before dinner at top Peranakan restaurant **Blue Ginger** (p72). Dinner done, catch a taxi to the atmospheric **Night Safari** (p136), slipping into the dark for a late-night rendezvous with a cast of majestic and curious creatures.

Day Two

After breakfasting at **Wild Honey** (p55), mall-crawl along shopping mecca **Orchard Rd** (p58). Hunt down rare Singaporean prints and books at **Antiques of the Orient** (p59) and edgy local fashion at **Blackmarket No 2** (p59). Shopped out, lunch at brilliant pan-Asian **Takashimaya Food Village** (p54).

Take in the architecture on heritage-listed **Emerald Hill Rd** (p52) before catching contemporary Asian art at **Singapore Art Museum** (p32). Then head to the Malay district, **Kampong Glam** (p84), home to golden-domed **Sultan Mosque** (p90), trendy **Haji Lane** (p102) and bespoke perfumery **Sifr Aromatics** (p100). Coffee and cocktail geeks shouldn't miss a swill at **Maison Ikkoku** (p97).

Heady, raffish and especially intense at night, **Little India** (p84) turns the Singapore stereotype inside out. Explore the jumble of street stalls, garland vendors and blaring Bollywood tunes on and off Serangoon Rd, pick up a sari at **Tekka Centre** (p96), then dig into mouthwatering north Indian and Nepalese grub at **Shish Mahal** (p95). Catch a Bollywood blockbuster at **Rex Cinemas** (p100), live tunes at **Prince of Wales** (p98), or go on a retail rampage at the 24-hour **Mustafa Centre** (p101).

Short on time?
We've arranged Singapore's must-sees into these day-by-day itineraries to make sure you see the very best of the city in the time you have available.

Day Three

☀ Beat the heat with an early-morning stroll along the **Southern Ridges** (p140). Opt for the 4km route from **Kent Ridge Park** (p141), through **HortPark** (p141) and across to Telok Blangah Hill Park, traversing the striking **Henderson Waves** (p141) walkway, before finishing at **Mt Faber** (p141). From here, it's a quick cable-car ride down to **Sentosa** (p110).

☀ Lunch on hawker-style grub at **Malaysian Food Street** (p117), then hit the squeal-inducing rides and movie-set streets of nearby **Universal Studios** (p112). If you're feeling brave, tackle the theme park's duelling roller coasters, reputedly the world's tallest.

☾ You could easily spend a full day at Universal Studios, but make time for sunset drinks at **Tanjong Beach Club** (p117) or predinner pampering at **Spa Botanica** (p118). Either way, crank up the indulgence with a little fine dining on the terrace at sleek, romantic **Cliff** (p116). If the night's still young, hit the dance floor at **St James Power Station** (p149) or head back into the city for some DJ-induced euphoria at **Zouk** (p41) or **Home Club** (p41).

Day Four

☀ Head to **Changi** (p108), reflecting on history's darker side at **Changi Prison Museum & Chapel** (p109) before catching a bumboat (motorised sampan) across to quaint, stuck-in-time **Pulau Ubin** (p108).

☀ Tuck into fresh seafood at one of the eateries around the Pulau Ubin pier, then rent a bicycle and pedal around the island to take in the tin-shack houses and lush jungle. Amble along the boardwalk at **Chek Jawa Wetlands** (p109) and peek into the surreal **German Girl Shrine** (p109). Done, sail back to Singapore in time to watch the sun set from sky-high **New Asia** (p38).

☾ Assuming you've made a reservation, it's time for a decadent degustation dinner at French-inspired, world-renowned restaurant **JAAN** (p35), perched 70 floors above the city. Request a table facing **Marina Bay Sands** (p170) for commanding views of the spectacular nightly light and laser show. End the night at gorgeous rooftop bar **Lantern** (p38) or join the crowds at **Clarke Quay** (p42) for a little late-night revelling.

Need to Know

**For more information,
see Survival Guide (p175)**

Currency
Singapore dollar ($)

Languages
English, Mandarin, Malay and Tamil

Visas
Citizens of the USA, UK, Australia, New Zealand, South Africa, Israel, most European countries and Asean nations (except Myanmar) do not require visas for stays of up to 30 days. Other visitors may require visas.

Money
ATMs are widely available and credit cards are accepted in all hotels and most restaurants.

Mobile Phones
Singapore's two cell networks (GSM900 and GSM1800) are compatible with most of the world. Buy a local SIM card to keep costs down.

Time
Singapore Standard Time (GMT/UTC plus eight hours)

Plugs & Adaptors
Square, three-pin plugs of the type used in the UK; current is 220V to 240V.

Tipping
Largely unexpected and unnecessary.

 **Before You Go**

Your Daily Budget

Budget under $100
► Dorm bed $16–$40
► Meal at hawker centre $3–$10
► Beer at street stall $5

Midrange $100–$350
► Double room in average hotel $100–$250
► Two-course dinner with wine $50
► Cocktail at hip bar $15–$25

Top end over $350
► Four- and five-star double room $250–$500
► Degustation menu at top-tier restaurant $250-plus
► Theatre ticket $150

Websites

Lonely Planet (www.lonelyplanet.com/singapore) Destination low-down, hotel bookings and traveller forum.

Your Singapore (www.yoursingapore.com) Tourist site with handy planning feature.

HungryGoWhere (www.hungrygowhere.com) Indie reviews by food-obsessed locals.

Advance Planning

Two months before Reserve a table at a top-tier restaurant; book tickets to the Formula One or to short-run, Broadway-style musicals.

One month before Book a bunk if you plan on staying at a dorm over the weekend.

One week before Scan the web for last-minute deals and upcoming festivals. Book a cabana at rooftop bar Lantern.

② Arriving in Singapore

Changi Airport (www.changiairport.com) is Singapore's major gateway. Easy connections to central Singapore via MRT train, public and shuttle bus 6am to midnight, $1.80 to $9*. Taxi ride $18 to $35, 50% more midnight to 6am, plus airport surcharge.

✈ From Changi Airport

Destination	Best transport
Colonial District, the Quays & Marina Bay	MRT
Orchard Rd	bus 36
Chinatown, CBD & Tanjong Pagar	MRT
Little India & Kampong Glam	MRT
Sentosa	MRT, then Sentosa Express monorail
Holland Village & Tanglin Village	Holland Village: MRT
	Tanglin Village: MRT, then bus 106
Southwest Singapore	MRT

*Although more expensive, a taxi from Changi Airport is by far the quicker option, no matter which part of Singapore you're staying in.

③ Getting Around

Public transport is efficient, safe and relatively cheap. Buy an EZ-Link card at MRT train station counters ($15) to save time and money. Cards are valid on both trains and buses.

Ⓜ MRT

Local metro. Easiest way to get around. 6am–midnight.

🚌 Bus

Covers MRT areas and beyond. 6am–midnight, plus a handful of night services.

🚕 Taxi

Safe, honest and relatively cheap. Flag one at taxi stands or try your luck on the street. Book ahead if travelling in peak hours. Hefty surcharges apply during peak hours and from midnight to 6am.

Singapore
Neighbourhoods

Holland Village & Tanglin Village (p120)
Leafy, moneyed, expat territory studded with designer delis and cafes, antiques stores and the orchid-laced oasis of the Botanic Gardens.

◉ Top Sights

Singapore Botanic Gardens

Southwest Singapore (p138)
Studded with gems, from precious art collections and wartime relics to jungle trails and a bizarre mythology theme park.

◉ Top Sights

Southern Ridges

Worth a Trip
◉ Top Sights

Singapore Zoo

Night Safari

Sentosa (p110)
Singapore's 'good time' island, with theme park rides and stunt shows, Ibiza-style beach bars, and the most decadent day spa.

◉ Top Sights

Universal Studios

Singapore Botanic Gardens ◉

Southern Ridges ◉

◉ *Universal Studios*

Orchard Road (p48)
Singapore's Yellow Brick Rd of retail, with malls, department stores and *Vogue*-approved boutiques, plus a heritage-listed street.

Little India & Kampong Glam (p84)
Little India's heady scents and street stalls, Kampong Glam's storybook mosque – this is Singapore at its most evocative.

National Museum of Singapore

Raffles Hotel

Asian Civilisations Museum

Chinatown Heritage Centre

Colonial District, the Quays & Marina Bay (p22)
Head here for historic and cutting-edge architecture, must-see museums and buzzing nightlife.

◉ Top Sights

National Museum of Singapore

Asian Civilisations Museum

Raffles Hotel

Chinatown, CBD & Tanjong Pagar (p62)
Incense-scented temples, raucous hawker centres, skyscraper bars and trendy restaurants in restored shophouses.

◉ Top Sights

Chinatown Heritage Centre

Explore
Singapore

Worth a Trip

Roof garden, Esplanade, designed by Michael Wilford –
Theatres on the Bay (p43)
KIMBERLEY COOLE/LONELY PLANET IMAGES ©

Explore

Colonial District, the Quays & Marina Bay

The Colonial District dazzles with its 19th-century buildings, A-list museums and sprawling malls. Just to the south, the sinuous Singapore River is where you'll find the Quays and their booty of restaurants, bars and clubs. East of here, the river spills into Marina Bay, home to megaresort, casino and entertainment-and-dining complex Marina Bay Sands. (Clarke Quay, p42)

The Sights in a Day

Spend the morning traversing the continent at the **Asian Civilisations Museum** (p26) before clearing your mind with a saunter along the Singapore River. Turn right at Coleman Bridge and continue your amble through soothing **Fort Canning Park** (p34). Once you're feeling peckish, it's time for lunch on the terrace at gorgeous **Flutes at the Fort** (p35).

Continue your cultural enlightenment at the **National Museum of Singapore** (p24), **Peranakan Museum** (p32) or **Singapore Art Museum** (p32), all within walking distance of Flutes. Clued-up, head to **Raffles Hotel** (p28) for an aperitif at the Bar & Billiard Room and a little wardrobe revamping at Front Row. Alternatively, ditch the museums for a stroll through **Gardens by the Bay** (p32) or a ride on the **Singapore Flyer** (p34).

Start the evening with a rooftop toast at **New Asia** (p38) or **Lantern** (p38), then spoil yourself with degustation delights at sky-high **JAAN** (p35) or enjoy simpler bistro fare at celeb-chef hot spot **DB Bistro Moderne** (p36). Either way, end the night with riverside drinks at the Quays, listening to live tunes at **Timbre@ Substation** (p44) or DJ-spun beats at **Zouk** (p41).

Top Sights

National Museum of Singapore (p24)

Asian Civilisations Museum (p26)

Raffles Hotel (p28)

Best of Singapore

Food
JAAN (p35)

Flutes at the Fort (p35)

Kilo (p37)

Jumbo Seafood (p37)

Royal China (p38)

Drinking
New Asia (p38)

Level 33 (p39)

Brussels Sprouts Belgian Beer & Mussels (p40)

Paulaner Bräuhaus (p40)

Getting There

M **MRT** City Hall (Red & Green Lines) and Dhoby Ghaut (Purple, Red and Yellow Lines) are the best MRT stops for the Colonial District. City Hall is connected via underground malls to Esplanade (Yellow Line). Raffles Place (Red and Green Lines) and Clarke Quay (Purple Line) serve the Quays. Marina Bay (Red Line) and Bayfront (Yellow Line) service Marina Bay Sands.

Top Sights
National Museum of Singapore

Imaginative, prodigiously stocked and brilliantly designed, Singapore's National Museum is good enough to warrant two visits. At once cutting-edge and classical, the museum ditches staid exhibits for lively multimedia galleries that bring Singapore's jam-packed biography to vivid life. It's a colourful, intimate journey, spanning Singapore's ancient Malay royals, colonial-era backstabbing, 20th-century rioting and reinvention, food, fashion and film.

◉ Map p30, D1

www.nationalmuseum.sg

93 Stamford Rd

adult/child $10/5

◷ 10am-6pm, Living Galleries to 8pm

Ⓜ Dhoby Ghaut

Don't Miss

History Gallery
Commencing with a dramatic, 360-degree video installation, the History Gallery offers an evocative multimedia journey through six centuries of Singaporean history. It's a trip that will have you peering into opium dens, eavesdropping on lunching colonial ladies and confronting harrowing tales of Japanese occupation.

Living Galleries
The 'living galleries' offer insight into modern Singaporean. Get the low-down on *wayang* (Javanese puppet theatre), hawker food culture, the link between fashion and women's rights, Singapore's celluloid history and intimate tales of family life.

Goh Seng Choo Gallery
Before his tenure as Singapore's first Resident and Commandant, Colonel William Farquhar (1774–1839) commissioned local artists to illustrate the flora and fauna he had discovered on the Malay Peninsula. These sumptuous watercolours now reside in the Goh Seng Choo Gallery, located beside the Living Galleries.

Art Installations
Seven quirky art installations pimp the museum's interior and exterior. Not to be missed are Kuhari Nahappan's *Pedas Pedas* (a giant bronze chilli on the lawn at the back of the museum) and Suzann Victor's swinging chandeliers, *Contours of a Rich Manoeuvre* (on the link bridge to the museum extension).

FELIX HUG/LONELY PLANET IMAGES ©

☑ **Top Tips**

▶ The museum screens monthly independent and art-house films as part of its World Cinema Series. Tickets cost adult/concession $9/7.40. Check the museum website for upcoming screenings. Book online at www.sistic.com.sg or by calling ☏ 6348 5555.

▶ Entry is free to the Living Galleries from 6pm to 8pm daily.

▶ A 3 Day Museum Pass (adult/family $20/50) offers unlimited admission to eight city museums, including this one. Passes can be purchased at the museum.

✗ **Take a Break**

For a casual bite, cup of coffee or cheeky slice of cake, head to the museum's **Novus Cafe** (☺10am-6pm).

For inspired Chinese dishes from one of the city's most prolific chefs, book a table at the museum's beautiful, antiques-laden Chef Chan's Restaurant (p36).

Top Sights
Asian Civilisations Museum

The remarkable Asian Civilisations Museum houses Southeast Asia's most comprehensive collection of pan-Asian treasures. Set over three levels, its 11 beautifully curated galleries explore the history, cultures and religions of Southeast Asia, China, the Asian subcontinent and Islamic West Asia. Prepare to lose yourself in millennia of ancient carvings, magical swords and glittering jewels and textiles. Add to this a revealing exploration of the Singapore River and top-notch temporary exhibitions, and you have yourself one seriously satisfying cultural date.

◉ Map p30, E4

www.acm.org.sg

Empress Pl

adult/child $8/4, half price after 7pm Fri

◷ 1-7pm Mon, 9am-7pm Tue-Sun, to 9pm Fri

Ⓜ Raffles Place

Old-time Chinese workers quarters

Don't Miss

Southeast Asia Galleries
Spanning everything from Hindu Buddhist kingdoms to hillside tribes and Javanese performing arts, the Southeast Asia galleries' treasures include burial pottery and burial bronzes dating back over 1000 years, and a spell-packed 'magic' bark book from 1930s North Sumatra.

West Asia Galleries
Highlights include a Chinese Qur'an, which fuses both Chinese and Islamic aesthetics in its design. Equally unusual is the small collection of calligraphic leaves from Turkey, which sees verses from the Qur'an delicately inscribed onto dried leaves.

China Galleries
Look out for the richly hued, late-18th-century *Three Votive Luohan Portraits of the Qing Court* and colourful procession paraphernalia for the Goddess of the Sea (Mazu) Festival. Giant wooden statues like the Ming-dynasty-era Giant Red Warrior on display were once commonly placed outside local shops to protect against thieves.

South Asia Galleries
Beautiful artefacts include the Chola bronze sculpture of Uma, and a 19th-century gold *kazhuthu uru*, an ornate wedding necklace. More macabre is a 17th- or 18th-century Tibetan ritual bone apron, made using human and animal bones.

Colonial Architecture
Indian convict labour constructed the museum's home, the Empress Place Building, in 1865 for colonial government offices. It fuses neo-Palladian classicism and tropical touches: timber louvred shutters and a wide shaded porch. The original building covers Southeast Asia and South Asia.

☑ Top Tips

▶ Free, volunteer-run guided tours of selected museum highlights depart from the lobby at 2pm on Monday, 11am and 2pm Tuesday to Friday, and 11am, 2pm and 3pm on weekends. There's an additional tour at 7pm on Friday.

▶ The National Heritage Board's 3 Day Museum Pass (adult/family $20/50) offers unlimited admission to eight city museums, including this one. Passes can be purchased here.

✗ Take a Break

Cross the river and head up to 33rd-floor restaurant Peach Garden (p75) for beautifully prepared Chinese dishes high above the city.

For a drink with a view, it's an easy walk across the river to gorgeous Lantern (p38).

![eye icon] Top Sights
Raffles Hotel

Yes, it's a cliché, but try resisting the allure of that magnificent ivory frontage, the Sikh doorman, and the echoes of Maugham and Conrad in the days when Singapore was a swampy, tiger-tempered outpost of the British Empire. Starting life in 1887 as a modest 10-room bungalow built by the Armenian Sarkies brothers, Raffles Hotel is today one of Singapore's most beautiful heritage sites, laced with quiet tropical gardens, nostalgia-inducing bars and even one of the city's hippest fashion boutiques.

◉ Map p30, F2

www.raffleshotel.com

Beach Rd

Ⓜ City Hall

Don't Miss

Raffles Museum
Tucked away on the 3rd floor, **Raffles Hotel Museum** (admission free; ⊙10am-7pm) heaves with fascinating memorabilia, including photographs, travel brochures and a city map from bygone eras.

Lobby
While the hotel lobby is technically reserved for 'residents only', smartly garbed visitors should be able to step inside. Slip into an armchair and soak up the 19th-century scene of white marble floors, teak staircase and hand-woven Persian rug, all awash in natural light.

Gardens
Raffles' lush gardens make for a soothing urban escape. The Casuarina trees in the Palm Garden were planted in honour of Somerset Maugham, whose book of short stories, *The Casuarina Tree*, is set in 1920s Malaya.

Front Row
Unisex boutique **Front Row** (www.frontrowsingapore. com; Shop 02-09, Raffles Hotel Arcade; ⊙noon-8pm Mon-Sat, to 5pm Sun) stocks cult local labels like I Am Who I Am, demisemiquaver, and Antebellum, foreign finds like French eco-activist fashion brand Cosmic Wonder, and accessories including handcrafted shoes, bags and satchels, and specially commissioned, artist-designed notebooks.

Chan Hampe Galleries
Pop into **Chan Hampe Galleries** (www.chanham pegalleries.com; Shop 01-20/21, Raffles Hotel Arcade; ⊙11am-7pm) for top-notch contemporary art. The emphasis is on established Singaporean artists, as well as cross-cultural, East-West projects.

☑ Top Tips
▶ It's a good idea to wear smart casual (including long pants and a collared shirt or T-shirt for men) if wanting to visit the hotel lobby or the Bar & Billiard Room.

▶ The best time to visit is late afternoon or early evening, when the heat softens, the tourist crowds are slightly thinner and the building is romantically spotlit.

✗ Take a Break
For an early-evening aperitif, ditch the overrated Long Room and chill out Raj style at **Raffles' Bar & Billiard Room** (⊙10am-late), which offers live jazz, a billiard table and a gorgeous verandah for languid lounging.

Postaperitif, head to Raffles' fine-dining Royal China (p38) for exquisite Chinese flavours in a powder-blue dining room.

Exeter Rd **A** Eber Rd

1

Killiney Rd

Lloyd Rd

Kim Yam Rd

3

Saiboo St Nanson Rd

B Penang Rd

Oxley Rise

Oxley

Walk

Jln Rumbia

Oxley Rd

2

Tank Rd

Mohamed Sultan Rd

Mohamed Unity St

Merbau Rd

Singapore River

Robertson Quay

Clemenceau Ave

Ord Bridge

Magazine Rd

Cumming St

4 Jln Minyak

Central Expressway

Havelock Rd

Havelock Square

5

Park Cres

Chinatown **M**

Mosque St

Pagoda St

Dhoby Ghaut **M** **C**

Fort Canning Rd

Canning Walk

Orchard Rd

D Prinsep St

Bras Basah Park

National Museum of Singapore

Fort Canning Tunnel **12**

Battle Box

Fort Canning Park **4** **5**

Fort Canning Reservoir

Col Tce

10

Peranakan Museum

1

35

Armenian St

Canning Rise

River Valley Rd

Read St

Ord Bridge

Read Bridge

21

14

Merchant Rd

MICA Building

33

41 **17** **30**

Clarke Quay **31** **36**

Clarke Quay **M**

Carpenter St

Hongkong St

North Canal Rd

Upper Pickering St

Hong Lim Park

Upper Hokien St Hokien St

Upper Cross St Cross St

Nankin St

China St Pekin St

Hill St **45** **40**

High St

8

Coleman Bridge

28 Elgin Bridge

South Bridge Rd

George St

Circular Rd

26

Reclining Figures

Church St

Phillip St

Eu Tong Sen St

For reviews see
- **⊙** Top Sights p24
- **⊙** Sights p32
- **⊗** Eating p35
- **◉** Drinking p38
- **★** Entertainment p41
- **⊞** Shopping p45

27

24 **37**

E
F
G
H

Bencoolen St

Rochor Rd

EW17

N 0   400 m
0   0.2 miles

Republic Ave

Waterloo St

Queen St

Queen St

Tan Quee Lan St

Liang Seah St

Victoria St

🗙 13

Republic Blvd

2 ◎ Singapore
Art Museum

M
Bras
Basah

North Bridge Rd

Bain St

Cashin St

Middle Rd

Purvis St

Beach Rd

Nicoll Hwy

MINT Museum
of Toys

Seah St

Yet Con

◎ 7

18 🏛

Raffles
Hotel

🔒 44

Temasek Ave Promenade

M

Marina
Promenade

Bras Basah Rd

Temasek Blvd

Stamford Rd

9 🏛

⭐ 34

City
Hall

M

🏛 20

Esplanade

M

🏛 25

Six
Brushstrokes

Raffles Blvd

🔒 46

🏛 43

City Link Mall

Civil War
Memorial
Park

Raffles Link

🔒 47

Coleman St

Colombo Ct

St Andrew's Rd

The
Padang

Connaught Dr

16

32 ⭐ 🔒 42

Raffles Ave

Singapore
Flyer

◎ 6

Esplanade Dr

Victoria Theatre &
Concert Hall

Esplanade
Park

Queen Elizabeth Walk

Anderson
Bridge

Cavanagh
Bridge

Esplanade
Bridge

Merlion
Park

Esplanade
Jetty

Helix
Bridge

East Coast Parkway

Asian
Civilisations
Museum

Boat Quay

Battery Rd

Collyer Quay

Fullerton Rd

⭐ 29

Marina
Bay

39

23 🔒 🗙 11

Gardens by
the Bay

◎ 3

UOB
Plaza

M Raffles
Place

🏛 19

15 🗙 🔒

38

MARINA
SOUTH

Marina
City
Park

Republic
Plaza

🏛 22

Sights

Peranakan Museum MUSEUM

1 ◎ Map p30, D2

Stylish, interactive and thoroughly engrossing, Singapore's newest museum stands as a testament to the Peranakan (Straits-born locals) cultural revival in the Lion City. Explore 10 thematic galleries for an insight into both traditional and contemporary Peranakan culture, from marriage and folklore to fashion and food. Artefacts include exquisite textiles, furniture and engaging multimedia displays. (www.peranakanmuseum.sg; 39 Armenian St; adult/child $6/3, entry 7-9pm Fri free; ◎1-7pm Mon, 9.30am-7pm Tue-Sun, to 9pm Fri; ⓜCity Hall)

Singapore Art Museum MUSEUM

2 ◎ Map p30, E1

Magnificently restored, the Singapore Art Museum houses a superlative collection of Southeast Asian art, with a strong emphasis on modern and contemporary art from Singapore and the broader Asian region. Expect everything from painting and sculpture to site-specific installations and video art. One highlight is the Wu Guangzhong gallery, which features a rotating exhibition of $70 million worth of art donated by the father of modern Chinese painting. (www.singaporeartmuseum.sg; 71 Bras Basah Rd; adult/child $10/5, entry 6-9pm Fri free; ◎10am-7pm Sat-Thu, to 9pm Fri; ⓜDhoby Ghaut, City Hall)

Supertrees, Gardens by the Bay

Gardens by the Bay PARK

3 ◎ Map p30, H5

Catapulting nature into the future, Gardens by the Bay is the latest blockbuster attraction at Marina Bay. At present, only the Bay Garden South section is open. Highlights here include striking sci-fi 'supertrees' and slinky state-of-the-art conservatories housing plants from endangered habitats. The Heritage Gardens are also fascinating, inspired by Singapore's multicultural DNA. Check the website for project updates. (www.gardensbythe bay.org.sg; 18 Marina Gardens Dr; gardens free, conservatories adult/child $28/15, aerial

STUART JENNER/ALAMY ©

Understand

Architecture

Despite the wrecking-ball rampage of the 1960s and '70s, Singapore lays claim to a handful of heritage gems. An ever-expanding list of ambitious contemporary projects has the world watching.

Colonial Legacy

As the administrative HQ of British Malaya, Singapore gained a wave of buildings on a scale unprecedented in the colony. European aesthetics dominated, from the neoclassicism of City Hall, the Fullerton Building and the National Museum of Singapore to the Palladian-inspired Empress Building, now home to the Asian Civilisations Museum. Another influence was the Italian Renaissance, its aesthetics echoed in the MICA building and Victoria Theatre. While many other buildings adopted these styles, they were often tweaked to better suit the tropical climate, from the porte cochère (large porch) of St Andrew's Cathedral to the porticoes of the former St Joseph's Institution, current location of the Singapore Art Museum.

Shophouses

Singapore's narrow-fronted shophouses are among its most distinctive and charming architectural trademarks. Traditionally a ground-floor business topped by one or two residential floors, these contiguous blocks roughly span six styles from the 1840s to the 1960s. The true scene stealers are those built in the so-called Late Shophouse Style, with richly detailed facades often including colourful wall tiles, stucco flourishes, pilasters and elaborately shuttered windows. Fine examples grace Koon Seng Rd in Katong. The subsequent art deco style, which ditched the tiles for minimalist, streamlined motifs, can be seen on Ann Siang Rd in Chinatown.

Singapore Now

Some international A-listers designed modern offerings. American IM Pei is behind the striking OCBC Building and silvery Raffles City; twin-towered Gateway is designed to look 2-D from any angle. Britain's Sir Norman Foster designed the Expo MRT station and spaceshiplike Supreme Court, while Japan's Kenzo Tange was consulted for Singapore's tallest building, the OUB Centre. A recent contributor is Israeli-born Moshe Safidie, whose Marina Bay Sands complex boasts a record-breaking 340m-long cantilevered platform, Skypark, that sits atop three soaring skyscrapers.

walkway $5/3; ⏱5am-2am, aerial walkway 9am-9pm; **M**Bayfront)

Fort Canning Park   PARK

4 ◎ Map p30, C2

Gothic gateways lead into this pleasant park, where gravestones from the old Christian cemetery are embedded in the brick walls. There's also a spice garden on the site of Raffles' original botanical garden, where hollowed-out coconut shells on sticks offer samples of various spices for tasting. Look for the archaeological dig, where under a wooden roof you can see the 14th-century Javanese artefacts that have been uncovered there.

Battle Box   HISTORICAL SITE

5 ◎ Map p30, C2

Site of the former headquarters of the British Malaya Command, Battle Box is now a museum recreating the last hours before the fall of Singapore to the Japanese on 15 February 1942, using reasonably lifelike wax figures and unsettling audio effects simulating the bombing. (www.legendsfortcanning.com/fortcanning/battlebox.htm; 2 Cox Tce; adult/child $8/5; ⏱10am-6pm; **M**Dhoby Ghaut)

Singapore Flyer   OBSERVATION WHEEL

6 ◎ Map p30, H4

Welcome to the world's largest observation wheel (beating the London

---

Understand
The Armenian Connection

To the surprise of many, one of Singapore's more illustrious minority groups is the Armenians. Indeed, some of the city-state's most famous icons have an Armenian connection: the *Straits Times* was cofounded by Catchick Moses (Movessian), Raffles Hotel was established by the Sarkies brothers, and Singapore's national flower – the Vanda Miss Joaquim – was named for Agnes Joaquim, who reputedly discovered the orchid. Singapore's first church, consecrated in 1836, was the Armenian Church of St Gregory the Illuminator, located on Hill St. Armenian merchants first arrived in Singapore in the 1820s, seeing lucrative business opportunities in the promising British colony. By the 1880s some 100 Armenian families called Singapore home. The Great Depression and the Japanese occupation proved a devastating blow for many Armenian businesses, leading a great number to seek brighter horizons in Australia. Yet their legacy lives on in Singapore's architecture, press, law and in street names like Armenian St, Sarkies Rd and Galiston Ave.

Eye by 30m). One of the key Marina Bay developments, the 30-minute ride delivers impressive skyline and South China Sea views. To get your money's worth, choose a clear blue day, or a clear night, when the view includes the twinkling lights of neighbouring Indonesia and Malaysia. (www.singaporeflyer.com.sg; 30 Raffles Ave; ⊙8.30am-10.30pm; adult/child $29.50/20.65; ⓂPromenade)

MINT Museum of Toys MUSEUM

7 ◉ Map p30, F2

Nostalgia rulz at this slinky ode to playtime, its four skinny floors showcasing 50,000 vintage toys. Expect everything from rare Flash Gordon comics and supersonic toy guns to original Mickey Mouse dolls and oh-so-wrong golliwogs from 1930s Japan. Stock up on whimsical toys at the lobby shop or celebrate adulthood with a stiff drink at the adjacent Mr Punch bar. (www.emint.com; 26 Seah St; adult/child $15/7.50; ⊙9.30am-6.30pm; ⓂCity Hall, Bugis)

MICA Building ART GALLERIES

8 ◉ Map p30, D3

Once famous for having the city's first electric lifts, this architectural pin-up is now better known for its collection of art galleries. Among them is **Art-2 Gallery** (www.art2.com.sg) and **Gajah Gallery** (www.gajahgallery.com), which both specialise in contemporary Southeast Asian work. (140 Hill St)

Local Life
(Public) Bus Tour
Take a trip on bus 14. A double-decker doing the east–west route, it skirts the southern edge of downtown on the seven-storey East Coast Parkway, offering striking views of the skyscrapers to the north and harbour to the south.

Eating

JAAN FRENCH $$$

9 ✗ Map p30, E2

Perched 70 floors above the city, intimate, chic JAAN is home to French chef Julien Royer and his show-stopping Gallic creations: think wild langoustine with fregola sarda, grey chanterelle, rosemary-smoked organic egg and black Périgord truffle. The set seven-course menu ($238, with wine parings $418) is a culinary revelation. Always book ahead, and request a window seat overlooking Marina Bay Sands for a bird's-eye view of the nightly lightshow spectacular. (☎9199 9008; www.jaan.com.sg; Swissôtel The Stamford, 2 Stamford Rd; ⊙Mon-Sat; ⓂCity Hall)

Flutes at the Fort INTERNATIONAL $$$

10 ✗ Map p30, D2

Shamelessly romantic, fine-dining Flutes sits in a 1908 bungalow on the edge of Fort Canning Park. While the location is reason enough to climb the wooden steps, the imaginative, mod-Oz

ArtScience Museum (p155), architect Moshe Safdie, Marina Bay

menu makes it a must for gourmands. If the budget permits, opt for the Chef's Table menu ($108), whose creative show-stoppers might include melt-in-the-mouth sea scallops with *kataifi* prawn roll, micro celery, nori cracker and chilli-lime dressing. Book ahead. (📞6338 8770; www.flutes.com.sg; Fort Canning Park, entrance via 23B Coleman St; mains $38-48; ⏱lunch & dinner Mon-Sat, 10am-5pm Sun; Ⓜ City Hall)

DB Bistro Moderne
FRENCH, MEDITERRANEAN $$

11 🍴 Map p30, G5

Singaporean outpost of French chef Daniel Boulud, this smart yet relaxed hot spot is the best of Marina Bay Sand's celebrity-chef eateries. Tuck

into seasonal comfort food like succulent seafood risotto and the decadent, pâté-de-foie-gras-stuffed burger. Choose from almost 30 wines by the glass, including drops from boutique, lesser-known wineries. It's a good idea to book ahead for dinner Thursday to Sunday. (📞6688 8525; The Shoppes at Marina Bay Sands, 2 Bayfront Ave; Ⓜ Bayfront, Marina Bay)

Chef Chan's Restaurant
CHINESE $$

12 🍴 Map p30, D2

Eponymous chef, sick of cooking for over 200 people in his large restaurant, closes shop and opens tiny restaurant with nine tables and a daily changing set menu. It's decked out with his exquisite, over-the-top antique furnishing, which pales in comparison to the food. He recently handed the reins to a disciple while he jaunts through China to collect recipes. The menu (but not the atmosphere) is less stuffy; there's now dim sum, and prices have tumbled. (01-06 National Museum, 93 Stamford Rd; dim sum from $4.80, set meals from $38; Dhoby Ghaut)

Kilo   FUSION $$

13   off Map p30, F1

While its location might be slightly off the radar – the 2nd floor of an industrial riverside building – gastro geeks know exactly how to reach this gem. Oozing a contemporary dinner-club vibe, it's famed for brilliant Italo-Japanese creations – think zucchini pancakes with goat's cheese and *ibérico* ham, or *unagi* (eel) and teriyaki linguine. Simplify your life by taking a taxi. (6467 3987; www.kilokitchen.com; 66 Kampong Bugis; mains from $28; dinner Mon-Sat; Lavender)

Jumbo Seafood   CHINESE $$

14   Map p30, C4

If you're lusting for chilli crab – and you should be – this is the place to indulge. The gravy is sublimely sweet, nutty, with just the right amount of chilli. Be sure to order some yeasty, fried *man-tou* (buns) to dip with. While all of Jumbo's outlets have the dish down to an art, this one has the best riverside location. One kilo of crab is enough for two. (6532 3435; www.jumboseafood.com.sg; 01-01/02 Riverside Point; dishes from $8, chilli crab around $48 per kg; Clarke Quay)

Pizzeria Mozza   ITALIAN $$

15   Map p30, G5

This dough-kneading winner is co-owned by New York culinary superstar Mario Batali. It's also one of the few celebrity eateries at Marina Bay Sands that won't have you mortgaging your house. While both the antipasti and soulful pasta dishes are good enough to appease the pickiest *nonnas*, the star turn is the wood-fired pizzas, with big, crispy crusts to die for. (www.pizzeriamozza.com; The Shoppes at Marina Bay Sands, 2 Bayfront Ave; pizzas $18-37, mains $25-36; Bayfront, Marina Bay)

My Humble House   CHINESE $$$

16   Map p30, F3

Humble is not the first word that comes to mind when you clap eyes on the outlandish decor (designed by Chinese artist Zhang Jin Jie) and set menus with names like 'Someone is Singing Behind the Mountain'. If you're longing for bold, contemporary Chinese dishes like steamed Boston lobster with Hua Diao wine topped with steamed dried scallop and egg, book yourself a table. (6423 1881; www.myhumblehouse.com.sg; 02-27, Esplanade Mall, 8 Raffles Ave; City Hall; set menus lunch $60-80, dinner $100-120;)

Coriander Leaf

FUSION $$

17 Map p30, C3

Cross-cultural experimentation is what you'll get at this highly regarded bistro. While the menu can be a little disorientating, its East-meets-West repertoire mostly works. Celebrate world harmony with the likes of lentil tagliatelle with coriander-chilli pesto, or perhaps you could go for pita chips and eggplant ratatouille, or grain-fed Angus rib-eye steak with kimchi rice and spicy oriental eggplant. Coriander Leaf also runs highly regarded cooking courses. (☏6732 3354; www.corianderleaf. com; 02-03, 3A Merchant Court, River Valley Rd; mains $25-40; ☺lunch Mon-Fri, dinner Mon-Sat; Ⓜ Clarke Quay; ✈)

◯ Local Life
Cult of Yet Con

Perpetually packed, **Yet Con** (Map p30, F2; 25 Purvis St; chicken rice $5.50; ☺10am-10pm; Ⓜ City Hall) has been serving up superlative Hainanese chicken rice since 1940. Don't come expecting designer decor or charming service. Just come for the chicken, which is tender, packed with flavour and served to faithful suits, old-timers and geeky, 20-something food nerds by stern-looking aunties. Don't be put off by the crowds – turnover is fast.

Royal China

CHINESE $$$

18 Map p30, F2

Tucked away on the 3rd floor of the Raffles Hotel Arcade, powder-blue-hued Royal China is another top choice for refined Chinese flavours. Beautifully presented, dishes include swoon-inducing lobster noodles, silky steamed bean curd with scallop and egg white, and – if booked one day ahead – stewed clay-pot chicken with ginger and shallot sauce. (☏6338 3363; 03-09, Raffles Hotel Arcade, 1 Beach Rd; mains $12-119; ☺Mon-Sat; Ⓜ City Hall; ✈)

Drinking

Lantern

BAR

19 🍷 Map p30, E5

Fifth-floor Lantern may be height challenged but it has no shortage of X factor. Surrounding a glittering mosaic pool, it's a seductive melange of frangipani trees, skyscraper views, DJ-spun house and well-mixed libations like the Red Lantern (Don Julio tequila with watermelon, cucumber, lime and Cointreau). Call three days ahead if you fancy a cabana. (Fullerton Bay Hotel, 80 Collyer Quay; ☺8am-1am Sun-Thu, to 2am Fri & Sat; Ⓜ Raffles Place)

New Asia

BAR

20 🍷 Map p30, F2

Martinis demand dizzying skyline views and few deliver like this sleek bar-club hybrid, perched 71 floors above street level. Style up and head in early to watch the sun sink, then strike a pose on the dance floor. The $25 cover charge on Friday and Saturday includes one drink...but with views like these, who's counting? (Swissôtel The Stamford, 2 Stamford Rd; ⊗3pm-1am Sun-Tue, to 2am Wed & Thu, to 3am Fri & Sat; Ⓜ City Hall)

Brewerkz
BAR

21 Map p30, C4

The first among Singapore's crop of microbreweries and still the biggest and arguably the best. The beers are uniformly superb, from the hugely popular India Pale Ale to the quirkier seasonal fruit beers, with a solid choice of American comfort grub to soak it all up. Best (or worst) of all, the earlier you arrive, the cheaper the drinks. (www.brewerkz.com; 01-05 Riverside Point Centre, 30 Merchant Rd; ⊗noon-midnight Sun-Thu, to 1am Fri & Sat; Ⓜ Clarke Quay)

Level 33
BAR

22 off Map p30, G5

Brews with a view are what you get at the world's highest 'urban craft-brewery'. While the food doesn't quite match the loftiness of its locale, the house-brewed blonde lager, pale ale, porter and stout go down as smoothly as the panorama over Marina Bay. (www.level33.com.sg; Level 33, Marina Bay Financial Tower 1, 8 Marina Blvd; ⊗noon-midnight Sun-Thu, to 2am Fri & Sat; Ⓜ Raffles Place)

Ku Dé Ta
BAR

23 Map p30, G5

While we don't think much of the cocktails up here (stick to beer or wine), the $20 price tag is well worth it for the jaw-dropping views from atop Marina Bay Sands. Don't forget to bring your camera and snap away at Marina Bay, the city sprawl and busy South China Sea. DJs crank up the atmosphere nightly, spinning anything from rock to R&B. (Skypark, Marina Bay Sands North Tower, 1 Bayfront Ave; ⊗11am-2am Sun-Thu, to 4am Fri & Sat; Ⓜ Marina Bay, Promenade, Bayfront)

Understand

The Singapore Sling

Granted, it tastes like cough syrup, but there's no denying the celebrity status of Singapore's most famous mixed drink. Created by Raffles Hotel barman Ngiam Tong Boon, the Singapore sling first hit the bar in 1915. It's said that the recipe was so prized that it was locked up in a safe at the hotel for years. The secret has long been out: 30mL gin, 15mL Heering cherry liqueur, 120mL pineapple juice, 15mL lime juice, 7.5mL Cointreau, 7.5mL Dom Benedictine, 10mL Grenadine, and a dash of Angostura bitters, shaken with ice, decanted into a highball glass and garnished with a cherry. In 2010 the *Straits Times* newspaper called upon Albert Yam, the great-grandnephew of the cocktail's creator, to judge the city's best Sling. Top of the list was hotel bar **ta.ke** (Map p30, A5; Studio M Hotel, 3 Nanson Rd; ☺6pm-1am Mon-Sat). Bottom of the list? The Sling's most famous venue, Long Bar at Raffles Hotel.

Brussels Sprouts Belgian Beer & Mussels   BAR

24 🚇 Map p30, A3

Cute and popular, this restaurant/bar lays the Belgian theme on heavy with mussels, Trappist ales galore and Tintin murals on the wall (the whole gang's there, down to Thomson & Thompson). Get indecisive over the hundred-plus beers on the menu. (www.brusselssprouts.com.sg; 01-12 Robertson Quay, 80 Mohamed Sultan Rd; ☺5pm-midnight Mon-Fri, noon-1am Sat, noon-midnight Sun)

Paulaner Bräuhaus   MICROBREWERY

25 🚇 Map p30, G3

Join dehydrated business types for frothy tankards of Munich lager, Munich dark brews and platters of sausage and cheese 'knacker' at this three-level, wood-and-brass microbrewery. Beers are served in 300mL, 500mL and 1L (where's the loo?) steins, with seasonal brews like Salvator, Mailbock and Oktoberfest beers adding to the temptation. (☎6883 2572; www.paulaner.com.sg; 01-01 Times Sq, Millenia Walk, 9 Raffles Blvd; ☺noon-1am Sun-Thu, to 2am Fri & Sat; Ⓜ City Hall)

Harry's   BAR

26 🚇 Map p30, D4

The original and best of the 31 Harry's branches, this classic city-slicker hangout gained moderate infamy as the haunt of Barings-buster Nick Leeson. Loosen your tie and toast to happy hour (till 8pm), the occasional live band or the free pool table. (www.harrys.com.sg; 28 Boat Quay; ☺11am-1am Sun-Thu, to 2am Fri & Sat; Ⓜ Raffles Place)

Entertainment

Zouk
CLUB

27 ⭐ off Map p30, A3

Globe-trotting clubbers know all about Singapore's hottest club, with its A-list DJs, massive dance floor and five bars. While weekends are reserved for the latest dance, hip-hop, electro and techno sounds, Wednesday is a retro affair of '70s, '80s and '90s tunes. The complex is also home to alfresco Zouk, avant-garde Phuture, boudoir-inspired Velvet Underground, hung with Andy Warhol and Keith Haring originals, and the chill-out Wine Bar. (www.zoukclub.com; 17 Jiak Kim St; ⏰ Zouk 10pm-late Wed, Fri & Sat, Phuture 9pm-late Wed, Fri & Sat, Velvet Underground 9pm-late Wed-Sat, Wine Bar 6pm-2am Tue, to 3am Wed & Thu, to 4am Fri & Sat)

Home Club
CLUB

28 ⭐ Map p30, D4

Wedged between Boat and Clarke Quays on the Singapore River, Home Club enjoys serious cred with music buffs. The resident DJ nights kick some serious 'A', with playlists ranging from house, electro and retro to drum and bass and psytrance. The venue is also known for its live pop and rock acts and Tuesday comedy night. (www.homeclub.com.sg; B1-1/06, The Riverwalk, 20 Upper Circular Rd; ⏰ 6pm-2am Mon-Thu, to late Fri & Sat; Ⓜ Clarke Quay)

Butter Factory
CLUB

29 ⭐ Map p30, F4

At 743 sq metres, Butter Factory's as huge as it is slick. Street art on the walls of Bump, the hip-hop and rhythm-and-blues room, betrays its young and overdressed crowd. Fash is its cool 'art' bar, and walls are plastered with colourful pop-art reminiscent of underground comics (yes, the ones you hid from mum). Check the website for cover charges. (www.thebutterfactory.com; 02-02 One Fullerton, 1 Fullerton Rd; ⏰ 7pm-1am Tue, to 3am Thu, 8pm-3am Wed & Fri, to 4am Sat; Ⓜ Raffles Place)

Zouk

Attica

CLUB

30 Map p30, C3

Attica has secured a loyal following among Singapore's notoriously fickle clubbers, modelling itself on New York's hippest clubs but losing the attitude somewhere over the Pacific. Locals will tell you that it's all about schmoozing in the chichi courtyard, where eye-candy party people have one thing on their mind. A $28 cover charge on Friday and Saturday includes two drinks. (www.attica.com.sg; 3A River Valley Rd, 01-03, Clarke Quay; ⏰5pm-3am Mon-Thu, 11pm-late Fri & Sat; Ⓜ Clarke Quay)

Crazy Elephant

LIVE MUSIC

31 Map p30, C3

If the remodelled Clarke Quay is a collection of eager-faced college kids, then this beery, blokey, graffitied rock dive is the crusty old-timer shaking his head. One of Singapore's oldest live-music venues, it's the place to ditch all that electronic nonsense and surrender yourself to some serious, loud, grunting rock and blues.

Understand
Quays of the City

The stretch of riverfront that separates the Colonial District from the CBD is known as the Quays.

Boat Quay (Map p30, E5) Boat Quay was once Singapore's centre of commerce, and remained an important economic area into the 1960s. The area became a major entertainment district in the 1990s, filled with tourist-targeted restaurants, bars and shops. The streets behind the main strip are infinitely more interesting, with local restaurants and somewhat seedy bars.

Clarke Quay (Map p30, C3) How much time you spend in Clarke Quay really depends upon your personal sense of aesthetics – those who love pastels will swoon, those who don't will cringe. Packed with bars, clubs and restaurants, the place is chock-a-block at night. The best ones invariably have the longest queues.

Robertson Quay (Map p30, A3) At the furthest reach of the river, Robertson Quay was once used for goods storage. Now some of the old *godown* (river warehouses) have been sexed up into flash members-only party spots, and bars, though it's quieter and more low-key than its counterparts downriver. You'll also find several savvy hotels and restaurants clustered around here.

(www.crazyelephant.com; 01-03/04 Clarke Quay; ☺5pm-1am Sun-Thu, 3pm-2am Fri & Sat; Ⓜ Clarke Quay)

Esplanade – Theatres on the Bay   THEATRE, CLASSICAL MUSIC

32 ⭐ Map p30, F3

Where to begin? In the outstanding Concert Hall, the world-class theatre or the host of smaller performance spaces? The Esplanade roused Singapore from its artistic coma and placed it firmly at the centre of the Asian arts world. There are more than a thousand performances here every year, some of which are free. Check the website for upcoming events. (☎6828 8377; www.esplanade.com; 1 Esplanade Dr; ☺10am-6pm; Ⓜ Esplanade, City Hall)

Zirca Mega Club   CLUB

33 ⭐ Map p30, C3

The lines out the door don't seem to faze the gorgeous young things trying to get into Zirca. Mash with the mainly 20-somethings under pulsating lights in Zirca (dance club) or Rebel (hip-hop arena). Admission ($16 to $30 depending on the night) includes two drinks. (www.facebook.com/zircaclub; 01-02 Block 3C River Valley Rd, The Cannery, Clarke Quay; ☺9.30pm-late Wed-Sat; Ⓜ Clarke Quay)

Willow Stream   SPA

34 ⭐ Map p30, F2

Soothe yourself silly at this sprawling luxury spa, complete with plunge pools, spa baths and aromatic steam rooms. Top-of-the-range treatments include herbal, algae and thermal mineral baths, body wraps and 11 types of massage (including 'travel recovery' and 'shoppers' relief' options). Complete your revival at the in-house salon, which offers hair styling, waxing, manicures and pedicures. (☎6339 7777; www.willowstream.com; Level 6, Fairmont Hotel, 80 Bras Basah Rd; Ⓜ City Hall)

Top Tip
Street Sculpture
If you like your art free and alfresco, the area offers a healthy crop of public sculptures by acclaimed local and international artists. At Boat Quay, UOB Plaza is home to Salvador Dali's *Homage to Newton* (Map p30, E5) and Fernando Botero's *Bird*. Further east along the Singapore River, Cavenagh Bridge is the place for Chong Fat Cheong's *First Generation*. Esplanade – Theatres on the Bay claims Han Sai Por's *Seed* sculptures (Map p30, F3), while further northwest, Millenia Walk harbours Roy Lichtenstein's *Six Brushstrokes* (Map p30, H3).

Timbre@Substation

LIVE MUSIC

35 ⭐ Map p30, D2

Young ones are content to queue for seats at this popular live-music venue. The food is of the lazy fried variety, but a daily rotating roster of local musicians keeps things interesting and the crowds distracted. (www.timbregroup.com; 45 Armenian St; Ⓜ City Hall)

G-Max Reverse Bungy & GX-5 Extreme Swing

THRILL RIDE

36 ⭐ Map p30, D3

Fancy being flung 60m skywards at over 200km/h? If so, get yourself strapped inside the G-Max metal cage and prepare for a breathless view (figuratively and literally). A few Clarke Quay beers might improve your courage, but your stomach mightn't agree. Less terrifying is the neighbouring GX5, which will have you swinging over the Singapore River at a (slightly) more merciful speed. (www.gmax.com.sg; 3E River Valley Rd; per ride $49; ⏲2pm-late; Ⓜ Clarke Quay)

Singapore Repertory Theatre

THEATRE

37 ⭐ Map p30, B3

Bigwig of the Singapore theatre scene, the SRT repertoire spans Shakespeare and modern Western classics to contemporary works from Singapore, Asia-Pacific and beyond. Recent coups include a season of Sam Mendes' *Richard III* staring Kevin Spacey. Although based at the DBS Arts Centre, productions are also held at Esplanade – Theatres on the Bay and Fort Canning Park. (☎6733 8166; www.srt.com.sg; DBS Arts Centre, 20 Merbau Rd; Ⓜ Clarke Quay)

Understand
Singlish, lah!

While Singapore's official languages are Malay, Mandarin, Tamil and English, its unofficial lingua franca is Singlish. Essentially an English dialect mixed with Hokkien, Malay and Tamil, it's spoken in a rapid, staccato fashion, with sentences polished off with innumerable but essentially meaningless exclamatory words – *lah* is the most common, but you'll also hear *mah, lor, meh, leh, hor* and several others. Other trademarks include a long stress on the last syllable of phrases, while words ending in consonants are often syncopated and vowels distorted. What is Perak Rd to you may well be Pera Roh to your Chinese-speaking taxi driver. Verb tenses? Forget them. Past, present and future are indicated instead by time indicators, so in Singlish it's 'I go tomorrow' or 'I go yesterday'. For more, check out the Coxford Singlish Dictionary on the satirical website **Talking Cock** (www.talkingcock.com).

PETER PTSCHELINZEW/LONELY PLANET IMAGES ©

Shoppes at Marina Bay Sands

Shopping

Shoppes at Marina Bay Sands

MALL

38 🔒 Map p30, G5

You'll find all the 'It' brands at this sprawling, glamorous mall, including runway royalty like Prada, Hermès, Miu Miu and Fendi. Most people visiting cloister themselves in the dungeonlike casinos, leaving the mall itself empty – good news if you're not a fan of Orchard Rd crowds. You'll also find an ice-free skating rink, celebrity nosh spots, and the world's first floating Louis Vuitton store.

(www.marinabaysands.com; 10 Bayfront Ave; M Promenade, Bayfront, Marina Bay)

Society of Black Sheep

FASHION

39 🔒 Map p30, G5

Located inside the Shoppes at Marina Bay Sands, this is a sassy, unisex boutique that stocks adventurous, cult labels like Sydney's cyber-punk-inspired Injury, London's rockster Bolongaro Trevor and Singapore's bold and geometric Yumumu. Accessories include striking artisan jewellery from up-and-coming Singapore designer Carrie K. (www.societyofblacksheep.com; B1-64, Shoppes at Marina Bay Sands, Bayfront Ave; M Promenade, Bayfront, Marina Bay)

Fountain of Wealth, Suntec City

Funan DigitaLife Mall   ELECTRONICS

40  Map p30, D3

Tech mall of choice for people who prefer to pay a bit more for branded products and cast-iron guarantees, rather than brave the aisles of Sim Lim Sq (p102). **Challenger Superstore** (www.challenger.com.sg; Level 6; ☉10am-10pm) is the best one-stop shop for all IT desires. (www.funan.com.sg; 109 North Bridge Rd; ⓂCity Hall)

Royal Selangor   GIFTS

41  Map p30, C3

If Uncle Jim has always craved his own personalised tankard, here's your chance to get it for him. But wait!

Malaysia's pewter masters aren't as uncool as you may think, with enough contemporary jewellery, cufflinks, frames and corporate gifts to appease the harshest of Uncle Jim's critics. (www.royalselangor.com.sg; 01-01 Clarke Quay; ⓂClarke Quay)

Esplanade Shop   SOUVENIRS

42  Map p30, F3

Head here for souvenirs your family and friends will actually like. Pick up anything from 'Little Red Dot' and 'I Heart Laksa' tees, to Warhol-esque Singapore notebooks, contemporary brooches and funky cushions. (shop 02-02 Esplanade – Theatres on the Bay, 1 Esplanade Dr; ⓂEsplanade, City Hall)

City Link Mall

MALL

43 Map p30, F3

Designed by New York's Kohn Pederson Fox, this seemingly endless tunnel of retail links City Hall MRT station with Suntec City and the Esplanade. It's a tempting means of escaping searing sun or teeming rain, and a comfortable way of getting into the city from the Marina Bay hotels. Sure, it's a little disorientating, but with all the fashion and food down here, who cares? (1 Raffles Link; M City Hall)

Suntec City

MALL

44 Map p30, G2

Vast and bewildering, Suntec has everything under the sun, plus 60 restaurants, cafes and several food courts. One of the biggest crowd-pullers is the **Fountain of Wealth**, which was once accorded the status of World's Largest Fountain (though not, you'll observe, Most Attractive) in the *Guinness Book of Records*. Scan the media for one of Suntec's regular themed 'fairs', where you can pick up substantially discounted items such as cameras, electronics and computer gear. (www.sunteccity.com.sg; 3 Temasek Blvd; M Promenade, Esplanade)

Granny's Day Out

FASHION

45 Map p30, D3

Retro fans will adore this hidden treasure, with its supercool, ever-changing selection of vintage clothes, shoes and accessories from the '60s to the '80s. Sorry guys, unless you're into cross-dressing, 90% of the stuff here is for women only. (www.grannysdayout. com; 03-25 Peninsula Shopping Centre, 3 Coleman St; 1-8pm Mon-Sat, 1.30-6.30pm Sun; M City Hall)

Peninsula Plaza

MALL

46 Map p30, E3

The shopping centre that props up the Peninsula Excelsior Hotel has seen better days, but it's one of the best hunting grounds in Singapore for sporting goods and secondhand camera gear. Among the tennis rackets, bowling balls and football shirts are plenty of unexpected and eccentric shops, from guitar repairmen to designer sneakers. The ground floor has several shops peddling all sorts of quality camera equipment, including Leicas. (5 Coleman St; M City Hall)

Peninsula Shopping Centre

MALL, ELECTRONICS

47 Map p30, E3

A 'Little Burma' of sorts, this '80s time warp offers floors crammed with Burmese grocery stores, and hole-in-the-wall Burmese eateries. There are moneychangers here, and Singapore's best-stocked camera store (though not necessarily the cheapest), Cathay Photo, on the ground floor. Next door you'll find several stores with displays packed with secondhand camera gear. (3 Coleman St; M City Hall)

Explore

Orchard Road

Shopping is Singapore's national sport, and Orchard Rd is its Olympic-sized training ground. Indeed, what was once a dusty road lined with spice plantations and orchards is now a 2.2km torrent of blockbuster malls, department stores and speciality shops; enough to burn out the toughest shopaholics. But wait, there's more, including drool-inducing food courts and a heritage-listed side street rocking with bars.

The Sights in a Day

☀ Breakfast at **Wild Honey** (p55), raid the racks at Hansel – also in **Mandarin Gallery** (p60), then head west along the south side of Orchard Rd, popping into **Depression** (p61) for more local threads, **Ngee Ann City** (p58) to browse books at Kinokuniya, and futuristic **ION Orchard Mall** (pictured left; p58) for macaroons at **TWG Tea** (p56). At the end of Orchard Rd, make a quick detour for **Antiques of the Orient** (p59), then head back east along the north side of Orchard Rd.

☀ For lunch, nibble, slurp and swallow Singapore's best *xiao long bao* (dumplings) at **Din Tai Fung** (p53), in ubersmooth mall **Paragon** (p60). Further east, step back in time on **Emerald Hill Rd** (p52), bag more hiptastic local fashion at **Blackmarket No 2** (p59), then change gear with a visit to the film museum, **Cathay Gallery** (p52).

☾ Begin with an aperitif at see-and-be-seen **KPO** (p56) or revolving **Top of the M** (p56), then savour the flavour at Euro-Japanese superstar **Iggy's** (p52). If you don't have a reservation (or the credit limit), squeeze into sushi bolthole **Wasabi Tei** (p55). Cap off the night with live tunes at **TAB** (p57) or languid sipping at **Que Pasa** (p56).

♥ Best of Singapore

Getting There

Ⓜ MRT Orchard Rd is served by no less than three MRT stations: Orchard (Red Line), Somerset (Red Line) and Dhoby Ghaut (Red, Purple and Yellow Lines). There's really no need to use other forms of transport to get here.

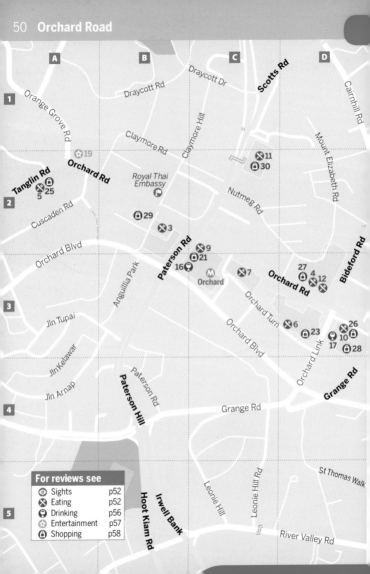

A Orange Grove Rd
Draycott Rd
Draycott Dr
Scotts Rd
B
C
D
Cairnhill Rd

Claymore Hill

Claymore Rd

★19
Tanglin Rd
Orchard Rd

⊗🅰25
5

Royal Thai Embassy

Mount Elizabeth Rd

⊗11
🅰30

Nutmeg Rd

Cuscaden Rd

🅰29
⊗3

Orchard Blvd

Paterson Rd

⊗9
🅰21
16

Ⓜ Orchard

⊗7

27
🅰 4 12
Orchard Rd

Bideford Rd

Anguillia Park

Orchard Turn

⊗6
🅰23

26
17 10
28

Orchard Link

Grange Rd

Jln Tupai

Orchard Blvd

Jln Kelawar

Paterson Rd

Paterson Hill

Jln Arnap

Grange Rd

St Thomas Walk

Paterson Rd

Hoot Kiam Rd

Irwell Bank

Leonie Hill

Leonie Hill Rd

River Valley Rd

For reviews see
- ◉ Sights   p52
- ⊗ Eating   p52
- 🅰 Drinking   p56
- ★ Entertainment   p57
- 🅰 Shopping   p58

E
F
G
H

▲ 0
Ⓝ 0   400 m
         0.2 miles

1

Peck Hay Rd

Monk's Hill Rd

Clemenceau Ave Nth

Cavenagh Rd

Bukit Timah Rd

Cairnhill Rise

Mackenzie Rd

Cairnhill Circle

Istana Park

2

Saunders Rd

Emerald Hill Road

Upper Wilkie Rd

Upper Wilkie Rd

Wilkie Rd

Cairnhill Rd

1 ◉

Emerald Hill Rd

Central Expwy

Buyong Rd

Edinburgh Rd

Sophia Rd

Hullet Rd

3

13 ⊙

Kramat Rd

Klok Rd

18 ⊙

⭐20

Kramat Ln

🔒22

24 🔒

Ⓜ
Somerset

14 ⊙

Orchard Rd

15 ⊙

Penang Rd

Oldham La

Cathay Gallery
◉ 2

4

Exeter Rd

Eber Rd

Oxley Rd

Handy Rd

Devonshire Rd

Killiney Rd

✕ 8

Oxley Rise

Clemenceau Ave

Penang La

Ⓜ Dhoby Ghaut

Lloyd Rd

Fort Canning Rd

Canning Walk

Fort Canning Park

5

Sights

Emerald Hill Road
HISTORIC AREA

 Map p50, E2

Take some time out from your shopping to wander up Emerald Hill Rd, lined with some of Singapore's finest terrace houses. Special mentions go to No 56 (built in 1902, and one of the earliest buildings here), Nos 39 to 45 (with unusually wide frontages and a grand Chinese-style entrance gate) and Nos 120 to 130 (with art deco features dating from around 1925). At the Orchard Rd end of the hill is a cluster of bars, including handsome Latino Que Pasa.

Cathay Gallery
MUSEUM

 Map p50, H4

Film buffs will go gaga at this cinematic museum housed in Singapore's first high-rise building. The displays here trace the history of the Loke family, early pioneers in film production and distribution in Singapore and founders of the Cathay Organisation. Highlights include old movie posters, cameras and programs that capture the golden age of local cinema. (www.thecathaygallery.com.sg; 2nd fl, 2-16 The Cathay, 2 Handy Rd; admission free; ⊙11am-7pm Mon-Sat; MDhoby Ghaut)

Understand
Thai'd to Tradition

With new shopping malls being shoehorned into every available space on Orchard Rd, why, many visitors ask, does the Thai embassy occupy such large, prominent grounds in an area of staggeringly expensive real estate? Back in the 1990s, the Thai government was reportedly offered $139 million for the site, but they turned it down because selling the land, bought by Thailand for $9000 in 1893 by the revered King Chulalongkorn (Rama V), would be seen as an affront to his memory. And so, happily, it remains, drooled over by frustrated developers.

Eating

Iggy's
INTERNATIONAL $$$

 Map p50, B2

What is arguably Singapore's best restaurant is now housed at the Hilton International after a long run at the Regent. The setting is swankier here, and the food as incredible as it always was: Japanese and European sensibilities meshed together in a tasting menu of epic proportions (eight courses for dinner!). The wine list is as impressive as it is extensive. (☏6732 2234; www.iggys.com.sg; Level 3, Hilton International, 581 Orchard Rd; lunch $85, dinner $195-275; ⊙lunch Mon-Fri, dinner Mon-Sat; MOrchard; ✐)

KEVIN CLOGSTUN/LONELY PLANET IMAGES ©

Emerald Hill Rd

Din Tai Fung
TAIWANESE $$

4 Map p50, D3

Even hype-resistant luminaries such as Anthony Bourdain have declared this chain the producer of the world's best dumplings (though some insist that only applies to the Taiwanese original). The signature *xiao long bao* are nevertheless sublime, the shrimp-pork wonton soup delectable, and the free-flowing jasmine tea a nice touch. There are 12 branches, including two others on Orchard Rd, inside Wisma Atria and 313 Somerset. (B1-03/06, Paragon Shopping Centre, 290 Orchard Rd; buns from $3.80, dumplings from $6.80; Ⓜ Orchard)

Bombay Woodlands
INDIAN, VEGETARIAN $$

5 Map p50, A2

Still one of the hidden gems of the Orchard area, Bombay Woodlands is below street level in the Tanglin Shopping Centre. The food is magnificent and cheap for this end of town: opt for the bottomless lunchtime buffet or order à la carte for south Indian classics like *idly* (spongy, fermented rice cake) or *dosa* (paper-thin lentil-flour pancake), washed down with a cooling lassi (icy yoghurt drink). (B1-01/02, Tanglin Shopping Centre, 19 Tanglin Rd; ☺10am-3pm & 6-10pm Mon-Fri, 10am-10pm Sat & Sun; dishes $5-14; Ⓜ Orchard; 🥗)

Food Republic

Takashimaya Food Village
FOOD COURT $

6 Map p50, D3

Prepare for some serious gut rumbling at Takashimaya's basement food hall. Slick, sprawling and heavenly scented, it serves up a *Who's Who* of Japanese, Korean and other Asian culinary classics. Look out for *soon kueh* (steamed dumplings stuffed with bamboo shoots, root vegetable *bangkwang*, dried mushroom, carrot and dried prawn), and don't miss a fragrant bowl of noodles from the Tsuru-koshi stand. (B2, Takashimaya Department Store, Ngee Ann City, 391 Orchard Rd; snacks from $1; ☺10am-9.30pm; Ⓜ Orchard)

Food Republic
FOOD COURT $

7 Map p50, C3

It's survival of the quickest when it comes to grabbing a table at peak times, but the mix of hawker classics, Thai, Japanese and Indian grub at Food Republic is well worth it. Make sure to stake a seat for yourself before joining the longest queues. Roving 'aunties' push around trolleys filled with drinks and dim sum, while the Waan Waan Thai stall does a seriously fine chilli-laced mango salad. (Level 4, Wisma Atria Shopping Centre, 435 Orchard Rd; ☺8am-10pm Mon-Thu, to 11pm Fri-Sun)

Killiney Kopitiam

COFFEESHOP $

8 Map p50, E4

A combo of white wall tiles, fluo-rescent lights and endearingly lame laminated jokes, this authentic coffee joint is a solid spot to tuck into a Singaporean breakfast of toast, soft-boiled eggs and sucker-punch coffee. Postbreakfast, devour staples like chicken curry, laksa or *nasi lemak* (co-conut rice, dried anchovies and spices wrapped in banana leaf), followed by a sweet-dumpling dessert. (67 Killiney Rd; mains $4-6; ⏱6am-11pm Mon & Wed-Sat, to 9pm Tue & Sun; Ⓜ Somerset)

Salt Grill

INTERNATIONAL $$$

9 Map p50, C2

Contemporary Australian flavours and 56th-floor views are what you get at Salt Grill, owned by renowned Aussie chef Luke Mangan. Survey the Singa-pore sprawl while nibbling on fresh fusion creations like tempura-battered king prawns with cucumber, papaya and a tamarind dressing. Alterna-tively, settle in at the bar for high-end tapas and a fab Pomelo martini. (☎6592 5118; www.saltgrill.com; 55-01 & 56-01 ION Orchard, 2 Orchard Rd; mains from $45; Ⓜ Orchard)

Wild Honey

BREAKFAST $$

10 Map p50, D3

Paging Tribeca with its faux brickwork, exposed plumbing and spotlights, Wild Honey peddles scrumptious all-day breakfasts from around the world,

from the tofu laced (Californian) to the *shaksouka* spiced (Tunisian). Other options include freshly baked muffins and cakes, gourmet sandwiches and rich, fresh roasted coffee. Get there before 9.30am on weekends or prepare to wait. You'll find a second, larger branch inside Scotts Sq mall, just off Orchard Rd. (www.wildhoney.com.sg; Level 3, Mandarin Gallery, 333A Orchard Rd; breakfast $12-24; ⏱9am-10.30pm Mon-Fri, 8am-10.30pm Sat & Sun; Ⓜ Somerset, Orchard; ⚲🤙)

Wasabi Tei

JAPANESE $$

11 Map p50, C2

Channelling 1972 with its Laminex countertop and wooden wall panels, this pocked-sized sushi joint feels like a scrumptious local secret. Stake a spot at the counter and watch the Chinese chef prove that you don't have to be Japanese to make raw fish sing with flavour. Note: decide on your order before sitting down as postorder amendments are not allowed. (05-70 Far East Plaza, 14 Scotts Rd; meals $10-30; ⏱closed Sun; Ⓜ Orchard)

PS Café

INTERNATIONAL $$

12 Map p50, D3

When all those Prada shopping bags start weighing you down, darling, re-fuel with the ladies who lunch at this ab-fab cafe. While we love the gour-met sandwiches, salads and pasta, the real reasons to come here are the stupendous desserts. Banana cream pie tops our list, or try the Key lime pie if you need a serious sugar hit. (www.pscafe.sg; 02-20/21, Paragon Shopping Centre, 290 Orchard Rd; ⏰9.30am-10.30pm; ⓂOrchard; 🖋)

Drinking

Que Pasa
BAR

13 Map p50, E3

For an evocative late-night swill, it's hard to beat this studiously raffish tapas and wine bar. Channelling old España with its tin lamps, strung chilli and El Pais wallpaper, its astute (if pricey) wine list is perfectly paired with succulent bites like anchovy bread. Its location on buzzing, heritage-listed Emerald Hill Rd is nothing short of perfecto. (7 Emerald Hill Rd; ⏰6pm-2am Sun-Thu, to 3am Fri & Sat; ⓂSomerset)

KPO
BAR

14 Map p50, F4

Stamps, cocktails and Lamborghinis: welcome to one of Singapore's quirkiest cocktail spots. Housed in a renovated postmaster's house, trendy KPO is as well known for its philatelic pedigree as it is for the luxury wheels of its see-and-be-seen evening clientele. Style up, order a cocktail, and scan the gorgeous rooftop terrace for your prospective ride home. (1 Killiney Rd; ⏰3pm-1am Mon-Thu, to 2am Fri & Sat, to 10pm Sun; ⓂSomerset)

Dubliners
IRISH PUB

15 Map p50, F4

Lousy Irish pubs filled with bellowing, beer-bellied execs are omnipresent in Singapore. Thankfully, this colonial-heritage beauty isn't one of them. Nurse your Guinness in the cosy gloom inside, or embrace the tropics on the alfresco verandah. The pub grub is well priced and tasty, and the service worth a little toast. (www.dublinersingapore.com; 165 Penang Rd; ⏰11.30am-1am Sun-Thu, to 2am Fri & Sat; ⓂSomerset)

TWG Tea
CAFE

16 Map p50, B3

Posh tea purveyor TWG peddles over 800 varieties of tea from around the world, from English Breakfast tea to Rolls Royce varieties like Da Hong Pao from Fujian. Savour the flavour with a few tea-infused macaroons – the *bain de roses* is divine. There's a smaller outlet one floor down. (www.twgtea.com; 02-20 ION Orchard, 2 Orchard Rd; ⏰10am-10pm; ⓂOrchard)

Top of the M
BAR

17 Map p50, D3

Rise above the retail madness at this revolving cocktail bar, located 137m above Orchard Rd. Peckish punters can order fine Chinese from 5th-floor restaurant Chatterbox (the chicken rice is especially good), otherwise order a well-earned libation and gaze north, south, east or west without ever leaving your seat. (Level 38, Orchard Wing, Mandarin Singapore; ☺5am–midnight Mon-Sat; Ⓜ Somerset)

Oriole Café & Bar   CAFE, BAR

18 🚇 Map p50, E3

In the caffeine wasteland that is Orchard Rd, slinky Oriole serves proper espresso, rich and fruity enough to placate most coffee snobs. Other libations include fresh juices, herbal teas and cocktails, while the bistro-style menu lines bellies with Euro comfort grub like *arancini* (fried porcini risotto balls), bangers and mash, and sticky pudding. (www.oriolecoffee.com; 01-01 Pan Pacific Serviced Suites, 96 Somerset

Rd, ☺11am–11pm Mon-Sat, 10.30am–11pm Sun; Ⓜ Somerset)

Entertainment

TAB   LIVE MUSIC

19 ⭐ Map p50, A2

One of only a few spots where local bands are encouraged to belt out their own stuff as well as covers. Foreign acts occasionally play here too. There are normally two gigs a night; the first starting at around 8pm, the second at around 11pm, although sometimes it's a DJ rather than a live band, and there are normally no live acts on

TWG Tea

Sundays. Many of the shows are free. Sometimes there's a cover charge (typically $20) that includes one or two drinks. (www.tab.com.sg; 02-29 Orchard Hotel, 442 Orchard Rd; ⏱9pm-5am Sun-Tue, 7pm-5am Wed & Thu, to 6am Fri & Sat; MⒸrchard)

Ngee Ann Foot Reflexology
MASSAGE

20 ⭐ Map p50, E3

This small, friendly and refreshingly unpretentious massage centre offers head, foot and body massages by visually impaired masseuses. If you're after luxe pampering, keep moving. If you just fancy a good, well-priced massage (treatments from $30), walk this way. (4th fl, Midpoint Orchard, 220 Orchard Rd; ⏱10am-10pm; MⓈomerset)

◌ Local Life
One Time, One Price

For a refreshing antidote to Orchard Rd's retail gloss, pop into time-warped **One Price Store** (Map p50, E3; 3 Emerald Hill Rd; ⏱10am-4pm; MⓈomerset). Tucked away in Peranakan shophouse on romantic Emerald Hill Rd, it's a time-warped antiques store brimming with Chinese art and antiques, including woodcarvings, porcelain snuff boxes and century-old embroidery. Some of the smaller items go for as little as $7 or $8.

Shopping

ION Orchard Mall
MALL

21 🔒 Map p50, C3

Curvaceous, high-tech and striking, Ion is Singapore's hottest (and most photogenic) mall, packed with both high-end couture and more affordable 'It' labels like Paul Frank, G-Star and True Religion. Shopped out? Recharge in the brilliant basement food court. The adjoining 56-storey tower comes with a top-floor observation deck, ION Sky. (www.ionorchard.com; 430 Orchard Rd; observation deck ticket counter level 4; observation deck adult/child $16/8; ⏱observation deck 10am-noon & 2-8pm; MⒸrchard)

313 Somerset
MALL

22 🔒 Map p50, E4

The new and hugely popular 313 has a great location above Somerset MRT Station and houses a cool, youthful mix of clothes shops, including Zara, Uniqlo, Mango, GUESS and much-loved local women's label m)phosis. You'll also find music stores, restaurants, cafes and the always-busy Apple shop, EpiCentre. Coffee lovers can get a decent fix at Oriole Café & Bar, just outside the west entrance. (www.313somerset.com.sg; 313 Orchard Rd; ⏱10am-10pm; MⓈomerset)

Ngee Ann City
MALL

23 🔒 Map p50, D3

Housed in a downright ugly, brown-hued marble and granite building,

Understand

Singapore Fashion Low-Down

Despite the glaring absence of the unorthodox and the preoccupation with ubiquitous international labels, Singapore is not without its batch of fresh, creative fashion makers. Top local names such as **Daniel Yam** (www.danielyam.com), **Anthea Chan** (www.perfectinblack.com) and **Nic Wong** (www.nicholasnic.com) are a match for any international label, while fellow A-lister Jo Soh of label **Hansel** (see p60) has carved an international reputation for her whimsical-yet-meticulous, affordable creations. Unisex hipster labels include minimalist **Feist & Heist** (www.feistheist.com) and the playful, irreverent Depression, the latter at **Cathay Cineleisure Orchard** (p61). Men-only standouts include studiously 'imperfect' **WanderWonder** (www.wanderwonder.com) and the stylishly eccentric Frederic Sai – the latter also at Cathay Cineleisure Orchard. Among the newer women's labels is geometric-obsessed **Demisemiquaver** (www.demisemiquaver.net). On Orchard Rd, head into **Blackmarket No 2** (p59) for an interesting handful of emerging local designers. Further east, **Raffles Hotel** (p28) is where you'll find Front Row, arguably Singapore's top spot for edgy, in-the-know homegrown labels.

Ngee Ann City redeems itself with seven floors of retail pleasure, where can't-afford luxury brands compete for space with the likes of **Kinokuniya** (www.kinokuniya.com.sg), Southeast Asia's largest bookstore, and Japanese department store Takashimaya, home to the mouth-watering Takashimaya Food Village. (www.ngeeanncity.com.sg; 391 Orchard Rd; ⏱10am-9.30pm; Ⓜ Orchard)

Blackmarket No 2 — FASHION

24 🔒 Map p50, E4

Hip, emerging Asian designers rule the racks at guys-and-gals Blackmarket No 2, among them Singapore's WanderWonder and Feist, the Philippines' Gian Romano, Black Heart and Anthology, and Indonesia's Rebirth. Pick up anything from graphic tees and whimsically detailed shirts to handcrafted shoes and jewellery. The store's centrepiece 'wooden shack' showcases a different designer every month. (www.theblackmarket.sg/blog; 02-10 Orchard Central, 181 Orchard Rd; Ⓜ Somerset)

Antiques of the Orient — ANTIQUES

25 🔒 Map p50, A2

Snugly set in a mall filled with Asian arts and crafts shops, Antiques of the Orient is a veritable treasure chest of original and reproduction vintage prints, photographs and maps from across the continent. Especially beautiful are the richly hued botanical

Paragon at Christmas

drawings commissioned by British colonist William Farquhar. (www.aoto.com.sg; 02-40, Tanglin Shopping Centre, 19 Tanglin Rd; ⏰10am-6pm Mon-Sat, 11am-4pm Sun; Ⓜ Orchard)

Mandarin Gallery MALL

26 🛍 Map p50, D3

After breakfast at Wild Honey, rehabilitate your wardrobe at this high-end, fashion-obsessed mall. Standout stores include Tokyo-based, boys-only **Bape Store** (www.bape.com), famed for its pop-meets-hip-hop-meets-preppy threads, sneakers and accessories in bold prints, luscious fabrics and playful detailing (think sweat-top hoods with 'monster' motifs). Female fashionistas shouldn't miss **Hansel** (www.

ilovehansel.com; 02-14), domain of local designer Jo Soh and her chic, playful, vintage-inspired creations. (333A Orchard Rd; Ⓜ Somerset, Orchard; 🛜)

Paragon MALL

27 🛍 Map p50, D3

Even if you don't have a Gold Amex, strike a pose inside the Maserati of Orchard Rd malls. The Shop Directory reads like a Vogue index: Burberry, Bvlgari, Gucci, Hermès, Jimmy Choo. Thankfully, mere mortals with a passion for fashion have a string of options, including Miss Selfridges, Calvin Klein Jeans, Banana Republic and Diesel. Rich or poor, head to PS Café and spoil yourself with a slice of

Top Tip
A Green Escape
When the retail fatigue creeps up on you, take solace in a rainforest. Believe it or not, you'll find one within 2km of Orchard Rd, within the grounds of the sublime Botanic Gardens (p122). So if you're longing for a green escape from the mall madness, hop on bus 7 or 77 from the Orchard MRT exit on Orchard Blvd and you'll be breathing easy in 10 minutes.

cake. (www.paragon.com.sg; 290 Orchard Rd; ⊙10.30am-9.30pm; Ⓜ Somerset)

Cathay Cineleisure Orchard
MALL

28 🅐 Map p50, D3

This Technicolor mall is packed with enough candy, bubble tea and *kawaii* (cuteness) to give pensioners pimples. That said, you'll also find some edgy local designers in here. Both men and women can push their boundaries at **Depression** (shop 03-05A); its playful, androgynous street-smart threads meld influences as diverse as Goth culture and kids' books. Guys should also check out the bold tees, shirts and knits at neighbouring **Frederic Sai** (shop 03-04B). (8 Grange Rd; Ⓜ Somerset)

Qisahn
ELECTRONICS

29 🅐 Map p50, B2

Gaming geeks swarm to this tiny in-the-know store. Famed for under-cutting the competition, it peddles both new and preloved video games in all major platforms, including Nintendo Wii, Sony Playstation, Xbox 360 and PC. You can check available games on its website, and don't forget – it will match any competitor's price. (www.qisahn.com; 05-12 Far East Shopping Centre, 545 Orchard Rd; ⊙noon-8pm; Ⓜ Orchard)

Exotic Tattoo
TATTOO SHOP

30 🅐 Map p50, C2

This is not just any tattoo shop – this is the domain of Sumithra Debi. Not only is she one of the few female tattoo artists in Singapore, she's the granddaughter of Johnny Two-Thumbs, Singapore's most legendary tattoo artist. Though there's another shop in the plaza bearing the Two-Thumbs name, Exotic Tattoo is the actual heir to the Two-Thumbs lineage. In addition to ink work, the shop also does piercing. (☏6834 0558; www.exotictattoopiercing.com; 04-11 Far East Plaza, 14 Scotts Rd; ⊙noon-9pm Mon-Sat, to 6pm Sun; Ⓜ Orchard)

Explore

Chinatown, CBD & Tanjong Pagar

This 'hood keeps things interesting with diverse architecture, culinary riches and buzzing bars. Not huge on must-see sights, it's about the vibe. Dive into Chinatown (pictured) for wet markets, hawker food, reflexology and temple-hopping, and into the CBD to dine atop skyscrapers. South of Chinatown, trendy Tanjong Pagar is great for contemporary galleries, single-origin coffee and heritage-listed shophouses.

Sights in a Day

☀ Breakfast at veteran **Ya Kun Kaya Toast** (p74), then get the dirt on the area's past at the **Chinatown Heritage Centre** (p64). Picture those opium dens as you saunter down Pagoda St to bursting-with-colour **Sri Mariamman Temple** (p70). Across the street, scour for antiques at **Far East Legend** (p80) and Chinese remedies at **Eu Yan Sang** (p80). Alternatively, treat yourself to a little pampering at **Kenko Wellness Spa** (p79).

☀ Hunt down a table at **Maxwell Road Hawker Centre** (p74) and taste-test the city's legendary street food, then lose yourself in the glittering excess of the **Buddha Tooth Relic Temple & Museum** (p70). Collect your thoughts on the peaceful rooftop garden, before making your way to **Yixing Xuan Teahouse** (p76) for old-school tea and nibbles.

☽ Come dinner, opt for spicy Nonya at **Blue Ginger** (p72) or tasty tapas at Jason Atherton's buzzing **Esquina** (p72). Either way, end the evening bar-hopping on Ann Siang Rd, making sure to drop in at **La Terrazza** (p76) for rooftop cocktails and at **Beaujolais** (p76) for a Gallic drop.

◉ Top Sights

Chinatown Heritage Centre (p64)

◯ Local Life

Chinatown Tastebuds & Temples (p66)

♥ Best of Singapore

Museums
Chinatown Heritage Centre (p64)
Baba House (p70)

Food
Blue Ginger (p72)
Maxwell Road Hawker Centre (p74)
Chinatown Complex (p75)

Drinking
1 Altitude (p76)
La Terrazza (p76)
Plain (p76)

Getting There

 **Metro** The MRT serves all neighbourhoods. Alight at Chinatown (Purple Line) for Chinatown, Raffles Place (Red and Green Lines) for CBD, and Tanjong Pagar (Green Line) or Outram Park (Purple and Green Lines) for Tanjong Pagar, including Duxton Hill.

🚍 **Bus** The 61, 145 and 166 link Chinatown to the Colonial District; bus 608 links it to Raffles Quay.

Top Sights
Chinatown Heritage Centre

Spread across three floors of three adjoining shophouses, the Chinatown Heritage Centre lifts the lid of Chinatown's chaotic, colourful and often scandalous past. While its production values can't match those of the city's blockbuster museums, its endearing jumble of old photographs, personal anecdotes and recreated environments deliver an evocative stroll through the neighbourhood's highs and lows. Spend some time in here and you can expect to see Chinatown's now tourist-conscious streets in a much more intriguing light.

Map p68, C2

www.chinatownheritage
centre.com.sg

48 Pagoda St

adult/child $10/6

9am-8pm

M Chinatown

Don't Miss

Roots Exhibition

At its simplest level, Chinatown was allocated to all Chinese traders in the Raffles Plan of 1828. Yet the area was further divided along ethnic lines: Hokkien on Havelock Rd and Telok Ayer, China and Chulia Sts; Teochew on Circular Rd, Boat Quay and Upper South Bridge Rd; and Cantonese on Upper Cross St and Lower South Bridge and New Bridge Rds. This section of the museum offers a look at these different groups, the trades they were known for, as well as an interactive board exploring the roots of common Chinese surnames.

Recreated Cubicles

The museum's faithful recreation of old Chinatown's cramped living quarters is arguably its best feature. Faithfully designed according to the memories and stories of former residents, the row of claustrophobic cubicles will have you peering into the ramshackle hang-outs of opium-addicted coolies, stoic Samsui women and even a hawker family of 10! It's a powerful sight, vividly evoking the tough, grim lives that many of the area's residents endured right up to the mid-20th century.

Recreated Tailor Shop & Living Quarters

The time travel continues one floor down, where you'll stumble across a recreated tailor shopfront, workshop and living quarters. By the early 1950s, Pagoda St was heaving with tailor shops and this is an incredibly detailed replica of what was once a common neighbourhood. Compared to the cubicles upstairs, the tailor's living quarters appear relatively luxurious, with separate quarters for the tailor's family and apprentices, and a private kitchen.

Local Life
Chinatown Tastebuds & Temples

Considering its past as a hotpot of opium dens, death houses and brothels, it's easy to write off today's Chinatown as a paler version of its former self. Yet beyond the tourist tack that chokes Pagoda, Temple and Trengganu Sts lies a still-engrossing neighbourhood where life goes on as it has for generations, at cacophonous market stalls, retro *kopitiams* (coffee-shops) and historic temples.

❶ Chinatown Wet Market

Elbow aunties at the famous **Chinatown Wet Market** (Chinatown Complex, 11 New Bridge Rd; ☉5am-noon), in the basement of the Chinatown Complex. At its best early in the morning, it's a rumble-inducing feast of wriggling seafood, exotic fruits and vegetables, Chinese spices and preserved goods.

2 Tiong Shian Porridge Centre

Appetite piqued, pull up a plastic stool at **Tiong Shian Porridge Centre** (265 New Bridge Rd; porridge $3.20-4.70; ⊙8am-4am), an old-school *kopitiam* where old uncles tuck into delicious congee. Winners here include porridge with century egg and pork, and the speciality claypot frog leg porridge. Each order is made fresh.

3 Chop Tai Chong Kok

Pick up something sweet at **Chop Tai Chong Kok** (34 Sago St; pastries from $0.50; ⊙9.30am-6pm), a supertraditional pastry shop in business since 1938. If you're undecided, opt for the speciality lotus-paste mooncakes. Once known for its sago factories and brothels, Sago St itself now peddles everything from barbequed meat to pottery.

4 Ann Siang Road & Club Street

A quick walk away is trendy Ann Siang Rd, well known for its restored heritage terraces and booty of restaurants, bars and boutiques. Architecture buffs will appreciate the art deco buildings at Nos 15, 17 and 21. Mosey along it and adjacent Club Street, also famed for its eateries, shops and architecture.

5 Ann Siang Hill Park

At the top of Ann Siang Rd is the entrance to Ann Siang Hill Park. Not only is this Chinatown's highest point, it's a surprising oasis of green in the centre of the city. Kick back on a bench, catch the skyline through the foliage and follow the walkways downward to Amoy St.

6 Siang Cho Keong Temple

Small, Taoist **Siang Cho Keong Temple** (66 Amoy St) was built by the Hokkien community in 1867–69. Left of the temple entrance you'll see a small 'dragon well': drop a coin and make a wish. The temple gets particularly busy at lunchtime when the faithful file in to offer incense and prayers.

7 Rafee's Corner

Time for a quick pit stop at **Rafee's Corner** (Amoy Street Food Centre, stall No 02-85, 7 Maxwell Rd; ⊙6.30am-6pm Mon-Fri, to 2pm Sat & Sun), a humble tea vendor inside Amoy Street Food Centre. If he's in a good mood, the owner might overexaggerate the pulling. This is your cue to laugh.

8 Telok Ayer Street

In Malay, Telok Ayer means 'Water Bay', and Telok Ayer St was indeed a coastal road until land reclamation efforts in the late 19th century. Among its famous residents is Al-Abrar Mosque, built in the 1850s, Thian Hock Keng Temple, the oldest Hokkien temple in Singapore, and the Nagore Durgha Shrine, a mosque built between 1828 and 1830 by Chulia Muslims from south India.

Havelock
Square

A

B

C

D

1

Hong Lim
Park

Pearl's Hill Tce

Upper Pickering St

Eu Tong Sen St
New Bridge Rd

Upper Hokien St

Park Cres

39

2

Pearl's
Hill
Reservoir

Pearl's
Hill City
Park

29

Chinatown

Upper Cross St

10

Chinatown
Heritage
Centre

Pagoda St 38

Mosque St

33

Pearl's Hill Tce

Temple St

24

Sri
Mariamman
Temple

Smith St

3

41

37

Club St

3

Pearl Bank

Eu Tong Sen St
New Bridge Rd

14

35

26 15
Sago St 16 36 19
28 30 18 20

Ann
Sian
Hi
Pa

Banda St

2

Ann Siang Hill

Outram
Park

Buddha Tooth Relic
Temple & Museum

Erskine Rd

Ann Siang Rd

31

CHINATOWN

12

Keong Saik Rd

Kreta Ayer Rd

Teck Lim Rd

23

Neil Rd

21 Murray St

Kadayanallur St

Singapore
City Gallery

5

4

Outram
Park

8
25

32

Murray Tce

Maxwell Rd

Chuan Rd

Duxton Hill

Cook St

Outram Rd

Bukit Pasoh Rd

27
9

Duxton Rd

Tanjong Pagar Rd

Peck Seah St

5

Neil Rd

22
40

7

6

Baba House

1

Craig Rd

South Bridge Rd

North Canal Rd

Circular Rd

Singapore River

Cavanagh Bridge

George St

Synagogue St

Boat Quay

Flint St

Church St

13

Chulia St

Bonham St

Battery Rd

Hokien St

Phillip St

Market St

UOB Plaza

Nankin St

China St

17 · Raffles Place

Collyer Quay

n Chew St

11

Pekin St

Amoy St

Telok Ayer St

Malacca St

D'Almeida St

Republic Plaza

Marina Bay

Cross St

Market St

Boon Tat St

Robinson Rd

oy

4 · Thian Hock Keng Temple

Cecil St

Telok Ayer St

Stanley St

McCallum St

Robinson Rd

Maxwell Link

MARINA SOUTH

Raffles Quay

34

Sights

Baba House MUSEUM

 1 off Map p68, A5

Baba House is one of Singapore's best-preserved Peranakan heritage homes. Period furniture has been added to original family photos and artefacts to create a wonderful window into the life of an affluent Peranakan family living in Singapore a century ago. The only way in is on a guided tour, held every Monday, Tuesday, Thursday and Saturday, but the tour is excellent and free. Bookings, either online or by telephone, are essential. (☑6227 5731; www.nus.edu.sg/cfa/museum; 157 Neil Rd; admission free; ⊙1hr tours 2pm Mon, 6.30pm Tue, 10am Thu, 11am Sat; ⓜOutram Park)

Buddha Tooth Relic Temple & Museum TEMPLE, MUSEUM

 2 Map p68, C3

Consecrated in 2008, this show-stopping, five-storey Buddhist temple is home to what is reputedly the left canine tooth of the Buddha, recovered from his funeral pyre in Kushinagar, northern India. While its authenticity is debated, the relic enjoys VIP status inside a 420kg solid-gold stupa in a dazzlingly ornate 4th-floor room. More religious relics await at the 3rd-floor museum, while the peaceful rooftop garden features a huge prayer wheel inside a 10,000 Buddha Pavilion. (www.

btrts.org.sg; 288 South Bridge Rd; ⊙7am-7pm, relic viewing 9am-6pm; ⓜChinatown)

Sri Mariamman Temple TEMPLE

 3 Map p68, D3

Originally built in 1823, then rebuilt in 1843, Singapore's oldest Hindu temple is most famous for its riotously colourful *gopuram* (entrance tower), built in the 1930s and featuring deliciously kitsch statues of Brahma the creator, Vishnu the preserver and Shiva the destroyer. In October the temple hosts the Thimithi festival, during which devotees hotfoot it over burning coals! (244 South Bridge Rd; ⊙7am-noon & 6-9pm; ⓜChinatown)

Thian Hock Keng Temple TEMPLE

4 Map p68, E4

Oddly, while Chinatown's most famous Hindu temple is swamped, its oldest and most important Hokkien temple is often a haven of tranquillity. Built between 1839 and 1842, it's a beautiful, serene place, and once the favourite landing point of Chinese sailors, before land reclamation pushed the sea far down the road. Curiously, the gates are Scottish and the tiles Dutch. (158 Telok Ayer St; ⊙7.30am-5.30pm; ⓜChinatown, Tanjong Pagar, Raffles Place)

Singapore City Gallery MUSEUM

5 Map p68, D4

This city-planning exhibition gallery provides a compelling insight into the

Understand
Peranakan Culture

Peranakan heritage has been enjoying renewed interest, mainly triggered by *The Little Nonya,* a high-rating 2008 drama series focused on a Peranakan family, and the opening of Singapore's outstanding Peranakan Museum (see p32). But who are the Peranakans?

Origins

In Singapore, Peranakan (locally born) people are the descendants of immigrants who married local, mostly Malay women. The largest Peranakan group in Singapore is the Straits Chinese. The men, called Babas, and the women, Nonya, primarily speak a patois that mixes Bahasa Malay, Hokkien dialect and English. The ancestors of the Straits Chinese were mainly traders from mainland China, their presence on the Malay peninsula stretching back to the Ming dynasty. The ancestors of Chitty Melaka and Jawi Peranakan were Indian traders, whose unions with local Malay women created their own unique traditions. All three groups are defined by an intriguing, hybrid culture created by centuries of cultural exchange and adaptation.

Weddings

No Peranakan tradition matches the scale of the traditional wedding. Originally spanning 12 days, its fusion of Fujian Chinese and Malay traditions included the consulting of a *sinseh pokwa* (astrologer) in the choosing of an auspicious wedding day, elaborate gifts delivered to the bride's parents in *bakul siah* (lacquered bamboo containers), and a young boy rolling across the bed three times in the hope for a male first-born. With the groom in Qing-dynasty scholar garb and the bride in a similarly embroidered gown and hat piece, the first day would include a tea ceremony. On the second day, the couple took their first meal together, feeding each other 12 dishes to symbolise the 12-day process, while the third day would see them offering tea to their parents and in-laws. On the *dua belah hari* (12th-day ceremony), the marriage was sealed and proof of the consummation confirmed with a discreet sighting of the stain on the bride's virginity handkerchief by the bride's parents and groom's mother.

Understand
Temple Tales

Before construction of the Thian Hock Keng Temple (p68) you see today, the site was home to a much humbler joss house, where Chinese migrants would come to thank Mazu, the goddess of the sea, for their safe arrival. Their donations would help propel construction of the current temple, the low granite barrier of which once served to keep seawater out during high tide. Look up at the temple's ceiling in the right wing and you'll notice a statue of an Indian-looking man, seemingly lifting a beam. The statue is an ode to Indian migrants from nearby Chulia St, who helped construct the building. During restoration works in 1998, one of the roof beams revealed a surprising find – a scroll written by the Qing emperor Guang Xu bestowing blessings on Singapore's Chinese community.

government's resolute policies of high-rise housing and land reclamation. The highlight is an 11m-by-11m scale model of the city, which shows how Singapore should look once all the projects currently under development are finished. (www.ura.gov.sg/gallery; URA Bldg, 45 Maxwell Rd; ⊙9am-5pm Mon-Sat; Ⓜ Tanjong Pagar)

Eating

Blue Ginger PERANAKAN $$

 6 Map p68, C5

A fashionable, homely shophouse restaurant dishing up all the rich, spicy, sour Peranakan favourites, including the *ayam panggang* (grilled chicken in coconut and spices) that is the restaurant's claim to fame. Other winners include the soulful *bakwan kepiting* (minced pork and crab meatball soup) and *sambal terong goreng* (spicy fried eggplant). Bookings recommended. (☎6222 3928; www.theblueginger.com; 97 Tanjong Pagar Rd; Ⓜ Tanjong Pagar)

Cumi Bali INDONESIAN $$

 7 Map p68, C5

Kitschy interiors meet authentic, mouth-watering Indonesian grub at this unsung gem. Tuck into flavour-packed staples like delicate *nasi goreng* (fried rice; opt for the lamb, not the chicken), grilled-to-perfection *sate madura* (a Javanese-style chicken satay) and the restaurant's namesake dish, consisting of grilled squid in a luscious, spicy paste. (www.cumibali. com; 66 Tanjong Pagar Rd; dishes $6.50-28; ⊙closed Sun; Ⓜ Tanjong Pagar)

Esquina TAPAS $$$

 8 Map p68, B4

Co-owned by UK Michelin-starred chef Jason Atherton, intimate, buzzing

Esquina has tongues wagging with its classic-with-a-twist Spanish morsels. Scan the paper placemat menu for standouts like the palate-shaking, wasabi-spiked scallops with ceviche and radish salsa, or melt-in-your-mouth Iberico pork and pâté de foie gras sliders, best devoured at the stainless-steel bar while swilling a sherry and chatting to the chefs. No reservations. (www.esquina.com.sg; 16 Jiak Chuan Rd; snacks $5.50-9.50, dishes $12-24.50; ⏱lunch Mon-Fri, dinner Mon-Sat; Ⓜ Outram Park)

Latteria Mozzarella Bar
ITALIAN $$

9 🍴 Map p68, B5

While we adore the leafy alfresco deck, strung with nostalgic tin lamps, the draw here is the buttery mozzarella. From *burrata* (cream-filled mozzarella) to *affumicata* (smoked), its many variations are flown in from Italy twice weekly to star in classic-with-a-twist dishes like stracciatella with eggplant caponata and pine nuts. Add crunchy bread and smooth Italian vino, and you too will be longing for Napoli. (☎6866 1988; www.latteriamb.com; 40 Duxton Hill; mains $25-35; Ⓜ Tanjong Pagar)

Hong Lim Complex
HAWKER CENTRE $

10 🍴 Map p68, D2

Not short on gossiping 'uncles' with discerning palates, this old-school food centre is routinely crowded – try the famous **Outram Park Fried Kway Teow** (Block 531A, 02-18; ⏱6am-4.30pm Mon-Sat), or head to **Hiong Kee Dumplings** (Block 531A, 02-37; ⏱8.30am-7.30pm) for the scandalously sublime Nonya *chang* (sweet pork dumpling with mushroom, sugared wintermelon and coriander) and Hokkien *chang* (pork dumpling with mushroom, chestnut and salted egg). (cnr South Bridge Rd & Upper Cross St; Ⓜ Chinatown)

Local Life
Art by the Docks

Culture vultures should check out Tanjong Pagar Distripark, an arts centre housed in dockyard warehouses near the now disused Tanjong Pagar Railway Station. The biggest hitter here is **Ikkan Art International** (www.ikkan-art.com; 01-05, Tanjong Pagar Distripark, 39 Keppel Rd; ⏱hours vary, check website; Ⓜ Tanjong Pagar), with past exhibitors including Chinese dissident Ai Weiwei and Japanese appropriation artist Yasumasa Morimura. For the hottest Southeast Asian artists, check out **Valentine Willie Fine Art** (www.vwfa.net; 02-04 Tanjong Pagar Distripark, 39 Keppel Rd; admission free; ⏱11am-7pm Tue-Sat, 11am-3pm Sun during exhibitions). Bus 145 from St Andrew's Cathedral, by City Hall MRT station, will get you there.

PAUL KINGSLEY/ALAMY ©

Trengganu St night market, Chinatown

Ya Kun Kaya Toast   COFFEESHOP $

11 Map p68, E2

Though it's now part of a chain, this airy, retro coffeeshop is an institution, and it's the best spot to start the day the Singaporean way. The speciality is buttery *kaya* (coconut jam) toast, dipped in runny egg (add black pepper and soya sauce like the locals) and washed down with strong *kopi* (coffee). The staff are friendly and there's outdoor seating to boot. (01-01 Far East Sq, 18 China St; kaya toast set $4; ☺7.30am-7pm Mon-Fri, 8.30am-5.30pm Sat & Sun; Ⓜ Chinatown, Raffles Place)

Maxwell Road Hawker Centre   HAWKER CENTRE $

12 Map p68, C4

One of Chinatown's most accessible hawker centres, Maxwell Road is a solid spot to savour some of the city's street-food staples. While stalls slip in and out of favour with Singapore's fickle diners, enduring favourites include **Tian Tian Hainanese Chicken Rice** (Stall 10; chicken rice $3; ☺11am-8pm Tue-Sun), **Maxwell Fuzhou Oyster Cake** (Stall 5; oyster cake $1.50; ☺9.30am-8.30pm Mon-Sat) and **Fried Sweet Potato Dumpling** (Stall 76; snacks from $0.50; ☺1-8pm Wed-Mon). (cnr Maxwell Rd & South Bridge Rd; Ⓜ Chinatown; ☝)

Peach Garden CHINESE $$

13 🍴 Map p68, F1

For a Chinese restaurant with a view, it's tough to beat this one. The food and service are immaculate too. Try to reserve a window table well in advance and tuck into superb dim sum, or equally sublime dishes like double-boiled chicken soup with sea whelk and fish maw, or stewed noodle with shredded pork, black fungus and bean paste. (📞6535 7833; www.peachgarde.com.sg; Level 33, OCBC Centre, 65 Chulia St; set menu from $38; Ⓜ Raffles Place)

Chinatown Complex HAWKER CENTRE $

14 🍴 Map p68, C3

Standouts at this labyrinthine hawker centre include **Lian He Ben Ji Claypot** (stall 02-082; dishes from $5; ⏱4-10.30pm Fri-Wed) and **Xiu Ji Ikan Bilis Yong Tau Foo** (stall 02-87/88; dishes $2-4; ⏱5.45am-3pm). The latter is famed for its dry *bee hoon* (vermicelli noodles), topped with crispy *ikan bilis* (dried anchovies) and accompanied by a bowl of *yong tau foo* (consommé soup) with optional add-ins like homemade fishcakes and tofu. (11 New Bridge Rd; Ⓜ Chinatown)

Ci Yan Organic Vegetarian Health Food VEGETARIAN $

15 🍴 Map p68, D3

Laid-back and friendly, Ci Yan peddles organic, flesh-free dishes in the heart of Chinatown. Scan the blackboard for the day's small selection of offerings, which might include golden curry puffs, durian Swiss rolls or wholemeal hamburgers. Our favourite is the brown-rice set menu, which comes with soul-coaxing Chinese vegetables and stew. (2 Smith St; ⏱noon-10pm; Ⓜ Chinatown; 🌱)

Tong Heng PASTRIES $

16 🍴 Map p68, D3

Hit the spot at this veteran pastry shop, locally revered for its melt-in-your-mouth egg tarts. Just leave room for the slightly charred perfection of the *char siew su* (BBQ pork puff). Oh, and did we mention the sublime coconut tarts? You have been warned. (285 South Bridge Rd; snacks from $1; ⏱9am-10pm; Ⓜ Chinatown)

⦿ Local Life
Bak Kut Teh Time

Singaporeans head just about anywhere for a good meal, so the positioning of famous *bak kut teh* (pork-rib soup) joint **Ya Hua Rou Gu Cha** (PSA Tanjong Pagar Complex, 7 Keppel Rd; soup $7.50; ⏱7am-3pm & 6pm-4am Tue-Sun; Ⓜ Tanjong Pagar) next to the port and beside an expressway doesn't stop the multitudes from coming to sip and swoon over peppery broth and gnaw on bones.

Drinking

1 Altitude
BAR

17 Map p30, G2

Fancy sipping cocktails perched on a cloud? This is the next best thing. Occupying the 63rd floor of the soaring 1 Raffles Pl skyscraper, it's a hypnotic combo of smooth lounge tunes, swaying palms and views of the glittering sprawl of Singapore and beyond. Dress up (no shorts or flip-flops) and don't forget your camera. (www.1-altitude.com; Level 63, 1 Raffles Place; ☉6pm-late; Ⓜ Raffles Place)

La Terrazza
BAR

18 Map p68, D3

The views across Chinatown and the CBD from this intimate rooftop bar, part of the hip Screening Room, are superb. Hunt down a comfy couch, kick off the shoes and have a shouting-into-each-other's-ears conversation over nostalgic '80s and '90s tunes. To reserve a bar table, call or email three days ahead. (www.screeningroom.com.sg; Level 4, 12 Ann Siang Rd; ☉6pm-1am Mon-Thu, to 3am Fri & Sat; Ⓜ Chinatown)

Beaujolais
BAR

19 Map p68, D3

A tiny, raffish bar perched on the corner of two trendy, bar-filled streets, Beaujolais is *très bon* for people-watching sessions. While we love the upstairs lounge, head in early for a terrace table and toast to the tropics over a glass of well-priced wine. (1 Ann Siang Hill; ☉noon-1am; Ⓜ Chinatown)

Le Carillon de L'Angelus
BAR

20 Map p68, D4

The excellent wines do justice to the superb tiled interior of this French wine bar. Lovely though it is upstairs, our favourite spot is the comfy chairs and sofa downstairs in a private little nook facing the chalkboard wine list. The cheese platter is a must. (24 Ann Siang Rd; ☉5pm-2am Mon-Sat, to 1am Sun; Ⓜ Chinatown)

Yixing Xuan Teahouse
TEAHOUSE

21 Map p68, C4

Banker-turned-tea purveyor Vincent Low is the man behind this venture, happily educating visitors about Chinese tea and the art of tea drinking. To immerse yourself more deeply, book a tea-ceremony demonstration with tastings ($20, 45 minutes). (www.yixingxuan-teahouse.com; 30/32 Tanjong Pagar Rd; ☉10am-9pm Mon-Sat, to 7pm Sun; Ⓜ Chinatown)

Plain
CAFE

22 Map p68, B5

A high-cred combo of stark interiors, neatly piled design magazines and Scandi-style communal table, The Plain keeps hipsters purring with Australian Genovese coffee, decent all-day breakfasts and sweet treats like lemon and lime tarts. Service is friendly and the vibe refreshingly

WIBOWO RUSLI/LONELY PLANET IMAGES ©

Chinese dragons, Chinatown

relaxed. (www.theplain.com.sg; 50 Craig Rd;
⏲7.30am-7.30pm; Ⓜ Tanjong Pagar)

Tantric

BAR

23 Ⓖ Map p68, B4

Black walls, gilded frames and a
palm-fringed courtyard define Singapore's hottest gay drinking hole. Especially heaving on Friday and Saturday
nights, it's a hit with preened locals
and eager expats, who schmooze and
cruise to Kylie, Gaga and Rihanna
chart toppers. Lushes shouldn't miss
Wednesday nights, where Wednesday
$20 gets you two martinis. (78 Neil Rd;
⏲8pm-3am Sun-Fri, to 4am Sat; Ⓜ Outram
Park, Chinatown)

Backstage Bar

BAR

24 Ⓖ Map p68, C3

While most of the look-at-me pretty
boys head to Tantric and Taboo, less
pretentious types gravitate here. Sit
on the balcony to chat and flirt with
local lads, or just sit back and watch
the world go by. Entrance on Temple
St. (13A Trengganu St; ⏲7pm-2am Sun-Thu,
to 3am Fri & Sat; Ⓜ Chinatown)

Oriole Coffee Roasters

CAFE

25 Ⓖ Map p68, B4

Eclectic lamps, communal tables and
a roasting room set the scene at this
serious coffee bolthole. Bean hunters
blog about the rich, fruity espresso,
while a very short, simple food menu

Top Tip

GLBT Singapore

As with many things, Singapore's stance on homosexuality is enigmatic. While homosexuality is technically illegal and lesbianism not even acknowledged, the gay, lesbian, bisexual and transgender (GLBT) scene exists, its handful of gay clubs, bars and saunas centred on Chinatown and Tanjong Pagar. Every August the gay community rallies around pride celebration **Indignation** (www.plu.sg/indignation). For updates on GLBT bars and events, check www.pluguide.com, www.fridae.com and www.utopia-asia.com.

includes eggs and toast, gourmet sandwiches and dainty sweets like custard cream puffs and strawberry butter cream cheesecake. Extended opening hours were planned at the time of writing. (www.oriolecoffee.com; 10/10A Jiak Chuan Rd; ⏰10am-6pm Mon-Fri; Ⓜ Outram Park; 🛜)

Wonderful Food & Beverage

DRINKS STALL

26 🚇 Map p68, C3

If you're fed up with the ridiculous prices for drinks in bars round here, head instead to this small, friendly street-side stall, grab a $5 beer and watch the Chinatown souvenir hunters whizz by. Extra perks include an interesting selection of exotic fruit drinks, as well as satay snacks. (6 Sago St; ⏰10am-10pm; Ⓜ Chinatown)

Toucan

PUB

27 🚇 Map p68, B5

With a pleasant garden area and a lovely location on the corner of the approach to cobblestoned Duxton Hill, this otherwise run-of-the-mill Irish pub is a decent choice for those who like their Guinness alfresco. Expect to pay at least $14 for a beer. (15 Duxton Hill; ⏰11am-1am Mon-Thu, 11am-2am Fri, 4pm-2am Sat; Ⓜ Outram Park, Chinatown)

Entertainment

Chinese Theatre Circle

CHINESE OPERA

28 ⭐ Map p68, C3

Teahouse evenings organised by this nonprofit opera company are a wonderful, informal introduction to Chinese opera. Every Friday and Saturday at 8pm there is a brief talk ($20, in English) on Chinese opera, followed by a 45-minute excerpt from an opera classic, performed by actors in full costume. Lychee tea and little teacakes are included in the price. Bookings recommended. For $35, turn up at 7pm and you can enjoy a Chinese meal beforehand. Search for Chinese Theatre Circle on Facebook. (📞6323 4862; 5 Smith St; Ⓜ Chinatown)

People's Park Complex   MASSAGE

29 Map p68, B2

Electronics, Chinese medicine, betting kiosks – this bustling, low-frills mall is Chinatown at its retro best. The real reason to come here is for the cheap massage places ready to vie for your body parts (opt for the busier ones). Our favourite is **Mr Lim Foot Reflexology** (03-53 & 03-78). Feeling adventurous? Try out one of the fish-pond foot spas on Level 3, where schools of fish nibble the dead skin right off your feet. (101 Upper Cross St; reflexology from $15; **M** Chinatown)

Screening Room   CINEMA

30 Map p68, D3

Get your ticket, order some Middle Eastern–inspired food and drinks, and sink into a comfy sofa to watch a film on a pull-down screen. Flicks span anything from Woody Allen comedies to celluloid classics like *Casablanca*. After the credits roll, pick at the plot at the rooftop bar. (✆6221 1694; www.screeningroom.com.sg; 12 Ann Siang Rd; ⊙noon-2.30pm & 6.30pm-late; **M** Chinatown)

Hood   LIVE MUSIC

31 Map p68, B4

The big draw at Hood is live music, played every night from around 9.30pm. It's mostly sing-along covers of Western chart-toppers, but the quality of the singers and bands tends to be decent and the atmosphere is pure fun. Beers go for $10, but you can get cheaper multibottle deals. (www.hoodbarandcafe.com; 55 Keong Saik Rd; ⊙5pm-1am Sun-Fri, to 2am Sat; **M** Outram Park, Chinatown)

Taboo   CLUB

32 Map p68, B4

After drinks at Tantric, cross the street and hit the dance floor at what remains the hottest gay dance club on the scene. Expect the requisite line-up of shirtless gyrators, dance-happy straight women and regular racy themed nights. (www.taboo.sg; 65/67 Neil Rd; ⊙8pm-2am Wed & Thu, 10pm-3am Fri, 10pm-4am Sat; **M** Outram Park, Chinatown)

Kenko Wellness Spa   SPA

33 Map p68, D2

Kenko is the McDonald's of Singapore's spas with branches throughout the city, but there's nothing drivethrough about its foot reflexology, romantic couples' sessions ($328 per 2½-hour session) or Chinese and Swedish massage (if you're after something forceful, Chinese is the way to go). (www.kenko.com.sg; 199 South Bridge Rd; reflexology per 30min $36, body massage per 60min $91; ⊙10am-10pm; **M** Chinatown)

Urban Fairways   VIRTUAL GOLF

34 Map p68, E5

Billing itself as Asia's first virtual-golf centre, offering players a virtual round on the world's top courses – all in air-conditioned comfort. Popular with corporate groups. (6327 8045; www.urbanfairways.com; Capital Tower, 168 Robinson Rd; off-peak/peak per hr $50/100; ⏱9am-midnight; Ⓜ Tanjong Pagar)

Toy Factory Theatre Ensemble

THEATRE

35 ⭐ Map p68, C3

A cutting-edge, bilingual (English and Mandarin) theatre company, Toy Factory Theatre Ensemble began its life

> ### Understand
> #### Speaker's Corner
>
> When Speakers' Corner (Map p68, D1) hit Hong Lim Park in 2000, the government and (government-regulated) press hailed it as a step forward for Singaporean freedom of speech. Notorious sticklers for novelty, 400 Singaporeans took to the stand in the first month to address the crowds. A year later only 11 stepped up. Now, it's completely deserted and, cynics will say, an accurate symbol of the state of free speech in a country whose attitude towards politics is predominately apathetic. Of course, you're still free to step up and state your mind...as long as you're Singaporean, register in advance with local police, avoid blacklisted subjects such as religion, politics and ethnicity, and stay within Singapore's sedition laws. Still feel like speaking out?

in puppetry. The group stages productions of well-known overseas plays as well as producing Singaporean works. (6222 1526; www.toyfactory.com.sg; 15A Smith St; Ⓜ Chinatown)

Shopping

Eu Yan Sang

CHINESE MEDICINE

36 🔒 Map p68, D3

Get your *qi* back at this venerable, user-friendly peddler of Chinese medicines and tonics. You can consult a herbalist for $12, or get off-the-shelf remedies such as instant bird's nest (to tone the lung) or deer's tail pills (to invigorate the kidneys). Most remedies also come with English instructions. (www.euyansang.com; 269 South Bridge Rd; ⏱8.30am-6pm Mon-Sat; Ⓜ Chinatown)

Far East Legend

ANTIQUES, HANDICRAFTS

37 🔒 Map p68, D3

Slip inside this small, charmingly cluttered shop for an excellent collection of furniture, lamps, handicrafts, statues and other objets d'art from all over Asia. Expect anything from dainty porcelain snuff boxes to ceramic busts of Chairman Mao. Best of all, the owner is usually willing to 'discuss the price'. (6323 5365; 233 South Bridge Rd; ⏱11.30am-6.30pm; Ⓜ Chinatown)

Utterly Art
ART

38 🔒 Map p68, C2

This small, welcoming art gallery is an excellent introduction to Singapore's contemporary art scene. It's mostly paintings, although sculpture and ceramics are exhibited on occasion, and roughly half of the displays are works from Singaporean artists. It also exhibits a lot of Filipino work. Call or check the website for what's on. (www.utterlyart.com.sg; Level 3, 20B Mosque St; ⏰noon-8pm Mon-Sat, to 5.30pm Sun; Ⓜ Chinatown)

Yue Hwa Chinese Products
DEPARTMENT STORE

39 🔒 Map p68, C2

This five-storey department store stocks everything Chinese, from porcelain teapots and jade jewellery to slinky silk cheongsams, dried fish and medicinal herbs, fungi and spices. Pick up some ginseng, a snakeskin drum or a jar full of sea horses for the road. (www.yuehwa.com.sg; 70 Eu Tong Sen St; ⏰11am-9pm; Ⓜ Chinatown)

Tong Mern Sern Antiques
ANTIQUES

40 🔒 Map p68, B5

Outside it's a beautifully renovated three-storey shophouse; inside, an Aladdin's cave of dusty furniture, books, records, woodcarvings, porcelain and a multitude of other bits and

Ⓠ Local Life

Paper, Death & Sago Lane

The curious paper objects on sale around Chinatown – from miniature cars to computers – are offerings burned at funeral wakes to ensure the material wealth of the dead. Veteran **Nam's Supplies** (Map p68, C3; www.namsupplies.com; 22 Smith St; ⏰8am-7pm) has been peddling such offerings since 1948, when nearby Sago Lane heaved with so-called 'death houses', where dying relatives were sent to spend their final days.

bobs – we even found an old cash register. A banner hung above the front door proclaims: 'We buy junk and sell antiques. Some fools buy. Some fools sell.' Better have your wits about you. (51 Craig Rd; ⏰9am-6pm Mon-Sat, 1-6pm Sun; Ⓜ Outram Park)

Yong Gallery
ANTIQUES

41 🔒 Map p68, D3

The owner here is a calligrapher, and much of his artwork is on sale. You'll also find jewellery, genuine jade products and antiques as well as more affordable gifts such as decorative bookmarks, Chinese fans and clocks. The shop is stuffed with goodies so it's fun to browse even if you're not in a buying mood. (260 South Bridge Rd; ⏰10am-7pm; Ⓜ Chinatown)

Local Life
Tiong Bahru

Getting There

Ⓜ **MRT** Catch the subway to Tiong Bahru, walk east along Tiong Bahru Rd for 350m, then turn right into Kim Pong Rd.

Spend a late-weekend morning in Tiong Bahru, Singapore's latest epicentre of cool. It's more than just an ever-increasing list of hip boutiques, bars and cafes that make this low-rise neighbourhood worth a saunter. This area was Singapore's first public housing estate, its streetscape of walk-up, art deco apartments now among the city's most unexpected architectural treats.

❶ Market & Food Centre

The **Tiong Bahru Market & Food Centre** (83 Seng Poh Rd) remains staunchly old-school, down to its orange-hued exterior, the neighbourhood's original shade. Its hawker centre is home to cultish **Tiong Bahru Roasted Pig** (02-38; ⏱7.30am-7.30pm) and **Jan Bo Shui Kueh** (02-05; ⏱6.30am-10.30pm), the latter famous for its *chwee kueh* (steamed rice cake with diced preserved radish).

❷ 40 Hands

Dive into **40 Hands** (www.40handscoffee.com; 01-12, 78 Yong Siak St; ⏱8.30am-6.30pm Tue & Sun, to 10pm Wed & Thu, to 11pm Fri & Sat) for a killer caffeine rush. One of the city's top coffee spots.

❸ BooksActually

Bibliophilic bliss, **BooksActually** (www.booksactually.com; 9 Yong Siak St; ⏱11am-6pm Mon, 11am-9pm Tue-Fri, 10am-9pm Sat, 10am-6pm Sun) is Singapore's coolest independent bookstore, with often unexpected choices of fiction and non-fiction, including vintage collectables.

❹ Strangelets

Strangelets (www.strangelets.sg; 7 Yong Siak St) is a beautifully curated design store filled with quirky local jewellery, French candles, Florentine soaps, Swedish socks, Californian bags and rucksacks. Try the orange and basil organic Popaganda popsicles.

❺ Nana & Bird

Around the corner is **Nana & Bird** (www.nanaandbird.com; 01-02, 79 Chay Yan St; ⏱noon-7pm Wed-Fri, 11am-7pm Sat & Sun). Originally a pop-up concept store, it's now a Tiong Bahru staple, with forward fashion, accessories and art. Find unexpected brands like Singapore's Aijek and By Invite Only.

❻ Ah Chiang's

Join gossiping uncles and Gen-Y hipsters for a little Cantonese soul food at **Ah Chiang's** (01-38, 65 Tiong Poh Rd; dishes from $3.50; ⏱7am-2pm & 6pm-midnight). The star turn at this retro corner *kopitiam* (coffeeshop) is fragrant, charcoal-fired congee. Do not go past the raw sliced *ikan parang* fish, delectably drizzled with sesame oil.

❼ Fleas & Trees

Ubercool vintage store **Fleas & Trees** (01-10, 68 Seng Poh Lane; ⏱6-10pm Tue-Fri, 10am-10pm Sat & Sun) occupies a converted cold storage. At the helm is Singaporean design professor Terence Yeung, who scours the world for fab men's and women's threads, decorative objects, eclectic plants and enough back copies of *Wallpaper*, *Vanity Fair* and *Vogue* to sex-up any coffee table.

❽ Orange Thimble

The **Orange Thimble** (www.theorangethimble.com; 01-68, 56 Eng Hoon Rd; sandwiches $7.50-8.50; ⏱11am-9pm Tue-Thu, 9am-10.30pm Fri & Sat, 9am-9pm Sun) is a cool cafe with little nooks and a steady stream of creative types, doubling as a gallery space. If you like your macchiato with a side of culture, stop by.

Explore

Little India & Kampong Glam

Little India (pictured above) is an un-Singaporean world where goods crowd the five-foot-ways, shophouses are the colour of crayons, and men in dhotis (loincloth) gossip over authentic *dosa* (savoury pancakes) at the marketplace. Walk 15 minutes southeast and you're in calmer Kampong Glam, dubbed Arab St. Head here for beautiful mosques, colourful fabrics, trendy boutiques and incredible street food.

The Sights in a Day

 Breakfast south Indian style at **Ananda Bhavan** (p93) then head north along colourful Serangoon Rd until you hit Hindu showpiece **Sri Veeramakaliamman Temple** (p90). Continue north to **Sri Srinivasa Perumal Temple** (p90), or go as far as bargain mecca **Mustafa Centre** (p101), and dive in for cut-price electronics, threads, shoes and jewellery.

 Recharge with Nepalese dumplings at **Shish Mahal** (p95), drop into the reputedly lucky **Kuan Im Thong Hood Cho Temple** (p91), then opt between bargain-hunting at **Bugis Street Market** (p101) or regional art at **Nanyang Academy of Fine Arts** (p90). Next stop: Kampong Glam. If you're not shopped out, hit fashion-literate **Haji Lane** (p102), otherwise head straight to whimsical **Sultan Mosque** (p90).

 Start off with a crafty cocktail at trendy **Maison Ikkoku** (p97), before some serious finger licking at **Nan Hwa Chong Fish-Head Steamboat Corner** (p92). Alternatively, dig into legendary *murtabak* (stuffed savoury pancake) at old-time favourite **Zam Zam** (p95) or Middle Eastern treats at **Café Le Caire** (p96). Cap your evening with late-night beers at boho classic **BluJaz Café** (p97).

 Local Life

A Stroll in Little India (p86)

Best of Singapore

Food

Warong Nasi Pariaman (p92)

Bismillah Biryani (p93)

Shish Mahal (p95)

Café Le Caire (p96)

Zam Zam (p95)

Tekka Centre (p96)

Drinking

BluJaz Café (p97)

Maison Ikkoku (p97)

Kerbau Rd Beer Garden (p98)

Prince of Wales (p98)

Shopping

Sim Lim Square (p102)

Mustafa Centre (p101)

Little Shophouse (p102)

Getting There

M Metro Little India is on the Purple Line. For Kampong Glam, walk 300m from Bugis (Green Line).

M Metro Farrer Park (Purple Line) is handy for the north end of Little India and Mustafa Centre.

Local Life
A Stroll in Little India

Loud, colourful and refreshingly raffish, Little India is everything Singapore is not supposed to be. Dive into a gritty, pungent wonderland of dusty grocery shops, gold and sari traders, haggling Indian families and heady Hindu temples. Jumble them all together with a gut-busting booty of fiery eateries and you have Singapore's most hypnotic, electrifying urban experience.

❶ Buffalo Road

Dive into subcontinental Singapore on Buffalo Rd. It's a bustling strip packed with brightly coloured facades, Indian produce shops, Hindu shrines and garland stalls. Flowers used to make the garlands are highly symbolic: both the lotus and white jasmine spell purity, while the yellow marigold denotes peace.

2 Tan House

As you walk up Buffalo Rd towards Serangoon Rd, look for an alley leading to Kerbau Rd on your left. Take a quick detour down it to be dazzled by Tan House. Sitting on the corner of the alley and Kerbau Rd, this is quite possibly Singapore's most colourful building. Once you've picked up your jaw, head back onto Buffalo Rd.

3 Tekka Centre Wet Market

If it's morning, slip into **Tekka Centre Wet Market** (cnr Serangoon & Buffalo Rds; ⏰6am-1.30pm), where locals battle it out for the city's freshest produce. It's an intense place, stocking everything from fresh yoghurt and dried curry spices to bitter gourds, black-skin chicken and halal meats. If you're after a sari, the top floor has an army of vendors.

4 Little India Arcade

Across Serangoon Rd lies **Little India Arcade** (48 Serangoon Rd), a little warren of shops peddling Indian saris, jewellery, sweets and handicrafts. Look out for **Jayaram's Creation** (shop 01-06/07), where henna tattoos cost from around $5. The arcade also houses the modest **Indian Cultural Corner** (admission free; ⏰9am-9pm), with old photographs and artefacts associated with the neighbourhood.

5 Thandapani Co

Slip into Dunlop St and look for **Thandapani Co** (124 Dunlop St). Adorned with hessian bags packed with chillies, fennel seeds and other Indian staples, this grocery shop is considered one of the city's best spice vendors, stocking ingredients you won't find elsewhere. It grinds its own spices and you can pick both savoury and sweet premixes.

6 Abdul Gafoor Mosque

Equally enticing is **Abdul Gafoor Mosque** (41 Dunlop St), with its intriguing mix of Islamic and Victorian architecture. Completed in 1910, it features an elaborate sundial crowning its main entrance, each of its 25 rays decorated with Arabic calligraphy denoting the names of 25 prophets. The sundial is the only one of its kind in the world.

7 Sungei Road Thieves Market

A ramshackle collection of tarpaulins and random junk, **Sungei Road Thieves Market** (Sungei Rd, Weld Rd, Pasar Lane & Pitt St; ⏰10am-6pm) offers a glimpse into the city's underbelly. Amid the sea of dusty laptops, cassette tapes and worn stilettos, you may just find a true gem, from Chairman Mao dinner plates to a Mont Blanc pen.

8 Sungei Rd Laksa

End your local experience with a cheap, steamy fix at **Sungei Rd Laksa** (Block 31, Kelantan Lane, Stall 01-12 Seng Chuan Eating House; laksa $2; ⏰8.30am-9pm). The fragrant, savoury coconut-base soup here enjoys a cult following, and only charcoal is used to keep the precious gravy warm. To avoid the lunchtime crowds, head in before 11.30am or after 2pm.

For reviews see	
☉ Sights	p90
⊗ Eating	p92
🍷 Drinking	p97
🎭 Entertainment	p99
🛍 Shopping	p100

Sights

Sri Srinivasa Perumal Temple
TEMPLE

1 ◉ Map p88, C2

Dating from 1855, this is one of the city's most important temples. If you visit in February for the Thaipusam Festival, the procession of devotees, with spikes and skewers driven through their bodies, begins under the temple's *gopuram* (entrance tower). (397 Serangoon Rd; ⏱ 5.45am–noon & 5-9pm; M Farrer Park)

Sri Veeramakaliamman Temple
TEMPLE

2 ◉ Map p88, B4

Little India's most colourful, bustling temple is dedicated to the goddess Kali, usually depicted wearing a necklace of skulls and disembowelling unfortunate humans. The bloodthirsty consort of Shiva has always been popular in Bengal, the birthplace of the labourers who built the structure in 1881. The temple is at its most evocative during each of the four daily *puja* (prayer) sessions. (141 Serangoon Rd; ⏱ 5.15am–12.15pm & 4-9.15pm; M Little India)

Sri Vadapathira Kaliamman Temple
TEMPLE

3 ◉ Map p88, D1

Dedicated to Kaliamman, the Destroyer of Evil, this south Indian temple began life in 1870 as a modest shrine, but underwent a significant facelift in the 1960s to transform it into the beautifully colourful structure you see today. The carvings here – particularly on the domed *vimana* inside – are among the best temple artwork you'll see anywhere in Singapore. (555 Serangoon Rd; M Farrer Park, Boon King)

Sultan Mosque
MOSQUE

4 ◉ Map p88, D6

Singapore's principal mosque and the spiritual focal point for the neighbourhood since the days when it was the embarkation point for Mecca-bound pilgrims. Magnificently crowned by a golden dome, the building (designed, interestingly, by an Irishman) dates from 1928, although a mosque has stood here since 1825. A constitution for the mosque stipulates that its trustees must include Malays, Javanese, Bugis, Arabs, north Indian Muslims and Tamils to represent the multi-ethnic nature of Singapore's Islamic community. (www.sultanmosque.org.sg; 3 Muscat St; ⏱ 9am–noon & 2-4pm Sat-Thu, 2.30-4pm Fri; M Bugis)

Nanyang Academy of Fine Arts
ART GALLERY

5 ◉ Map p88, B7

For a peek at work being turned out by artists in Singapore and elsewhere in the region, stop by the galleries inside this leading Singaporean art school. The rotating exhibitions focus on both established artists and emerging talent, in genres including

Sultan Mosque

painting, sculpture, photography and contemporary design. Best of all, admission is free. (www.nafa.edu.sg; 80 Bencoolen St; admission free; ⊗11am-7pm Tue-Sun; Ⓜ Bras Basah, Bugis)

Kuan Im Thong Hood Cho Temple TEMPLE

 6 ⊚ Map p88, B7

Dedicated to Kuan Yin, goddess of mercy, this is one of Singapore's busiest temples. Flower sellers, fortune tellers and incense-wielding devotees swarm around the entrance, the latter also rubbing the belly of the large bronze Buddha Maitreya nearby. (178 Waterloo St; ⊗6am-6.15pm; Ⓜ Bugis)

Malay Heritage Centre MUSEUM

7 ⊚ Map p88, E6

The Kampong Glam area is the historic seat of the Malay royalty, resident here before the arrival of Raffles, and the *istana* (palace) on this site was built for the last sultan of Singapore, Ali Iskander Shah, between 1836 and 1843. It's now a museum, offering an interesting account of Singapore's Malay people. The museum recently underwent renovations but should have reopened by the time you read this. (www.malayheritage.org.sg; 85 Sultan Gate; adult/child $3/2; ⊗10am-6pm Tue-Sun, 1-6pm Mon; Ⓜ Bugis)

Top Tip

Little India, Full Force

If you want to see Little India at its busiest Indian best, head in on a Sunday. This is the only day off for many workers, particularly Indian labourers, and by late afternoon you'll feel like you're sharing the streets with half the subcontinent.

Children Little Museum   MUSEUM

 8   Map p88, E6

This delightful personal collection of retro toys showcases how kids in Singapore once lived without games consoles. Wonderfully enthusiastic owner Terry Chua will take you on a private tour of the museum, bringing to life the toys on show with tales of how he and his friends used to play with them. There are also a number of toys for sale. (42 Bussorah St; admission $2, toy-making workshops $15; ⏲11am-6pm; Ⓜ Bugis)

Eating

Warong Nasi Pariaman   MALAY, INDONESIAN $

 9   Map p88, D6

With fans including former Malaysian prime minister Dr Mahathir Mohamad (that's him on the wall), this no-frills *nasi padang* (rice and accompanying vegetable dish) stall is the stuff of legend. Don't miss the *belado* (fried mackerel in a slow-cooked chilli, onion and vinegar sauce), delicate *rendang* (spicy coconut curry) beef, or *ayam bakar* (grilled chicken with coconut sauce). Get here by 11am to avoid the hordes. And be warned: most of it sells out by 1pm. (738 North Bridge Rd; dishes $2.60-4.60; ⏲7.30am-2.30pm Mon-Sat; Ⓜ Bugis)

Nan Hwa Chong Fish-Head Steamboat Corner   CHINESE HOTPOT $$

 10   Map p88, E5

If you only try fish-head steamboat once, you'd do well to make it at this hawker-style legend. The fish head is brought to you in the steaming broth of a large conical-shaped pot and is then shared by everyone at the table. One is enough for three or four people, and can stretch to more with rice and side dishes. There are four types of fish to choose from – go for the fleshier red snapper ($20). (812-816 North Bridge Rd; fish steamboats from $18; ⏲4.30pm-12.30am; Ⓜ Lavender)

QS269 Food House   HAWKER CENTRE $

11   Map p88, B7

This is not so much a 'food house' as a loud, packed undercover laneway lined with legendary street-food stalls. Work up a sweat with a bowl of award-winning coconut curry noodle soup from **Ah Heng Curry Chicken**

Bee Hoon Mee (🕙8am-5pm Sat-Thu) or join the queue at the equally cultish **New Rong Liang Ge Cantonese Roast Duck Boiled Soup** (🕙9am-8pm), with succulent roast duck dishes that draw foodies from across the city. (Block 269b, 269 Queen St; Ⓜ Bugis)

Bismillah Biryani INDIAN $

12 🍴 Map p88, B5

If you fancy savouring Singapore's best biryani, look no further. While the mutton biryani is the speciality – and it is special – even that is surpassed by the mutton *sheekh kebab,* which is a melt-in-the-mouth revelation. Just don't leave it too late in the day to get here, as most of the best stuff is long gone before 8pm. (50 Dunlop St; kebabs from $4, biryani from $6; 🕙noon-8pm; Ⓜ Little India)

Ananda Bhavan VEGETARIAN $

13 🍴 Map p88, A5

This supercheap chain restaurant is a top spot to sample South Indian breakfast staples like *idly* (spongy, round, fermented rice cakes) and *dosa* (South Indian savoury pancakes; spelt 'thosai' on the menu). It also does great-value thali (rice plate), some of which are served on banana leaves. You'll find other Little India outlets at 58 Serangoon Rd and 95 Syed Alwi Rd, as well as an outlet at Changi Airport's Terminal 2. (Block 663, 01-10 Buffalo Rd; 🕙6.30am-10.30pm; Ⓜ Little India; 🖉)

Sankranti INDIAN $

14 🍴 Map p88, C3

Specialising in food from the South Indian state of Andhra Pradesh, this is arguably the best of a cluster of good restaurants in and around Little India's 24-hour shopping hub, the Mustafa Centre. The extensive menu includes a number of north Indian dishes, too, and has a lip-smacking choice of set-meal thalis, the pick of the bunch being the Sankranti Special, a 10-piece culinary extravaganza. (100 Syed Alwi Rd; mains from $8; 🕙11.30am-4pm & 6pm-midnight; Ⓜ Little India)

LOOK DIE BILDAGENTUR DER FOTOGRAFEN GMBH/ALAMY ©

Cinnamon sticks

Understand

The Singaporean Table

Food is one of Singapore's greatest selling points, its medley of different cultures creating an international repertoire of local flavours.

Chinese

Thank the Hainanese for Hainanese chicken rice (steamed fowl and rice cooked in chicken stock, served with a clear soup and a chilli-ginger dip), and the Hokkiens for hearty *hokkien mee* (yellow Hokkien noodles with prawns) and *char kway teow* (stir-fried noodles with cockles, Chinese sausage and dark sauce). Teochew cuisine includes rice porridge, served with fish, pork or frog, while Cantonese classics include *won ton* soup.

Malaysian & Indonesian

Similar in style, Malay and Indonesian dishes also play a dominant role on the culinary scene. Feast on Katong laksa (spicy coconut curry broth with noodles, prawns, cockles, fish cake, bean sprouts and laksa leaf), *ikan assam* (fried fish in a sour tamarind curry) and *nasi lemak* (coconut rice with fried fish and peanuts). Equally mouth-watering is *nasi padang*, which sees steamed rice paired with a choice of meat and vegetable dishes like *sambal tofu-tempeh* (spicy tofu and fermented beans).

Peranakan

Peranakan (Nonya) food is a cross-cultural fusion of Chinese and Malay influences. Dishes are tangy, spicy and commonly flavoured with chillies, shallots, *belacan* (Malay fermented prawn paste), preserved soya beans, peanuts, coconut milk and galangal (a gingerlike root). Drool over *otak otak* (a sausagelike blend of fish, coconut milk, chilli paste, galangal and herbs grilled in a banana leaf) and *loh bak* (five-spice marinated pork wrapped in bean curd skin).

Indian

South India's hot flavours dominate. Tuck into thali (rice plate), a combination of rice, vegetable curries, *rasam* (hot, sour soup) and dessert served on a large banana leaf. Leave room for *roti prata* (fried flat bread served with a curry sauce), *masala dosa* (thin pancake filled with spiced potatoes and chutney) and halal (Muslim) *murtabak* (lightly grilled dough stuffed with onion and seasoned meat, usually mutton).

Tekka Centre (p96)

Shish Mahal

INDIAN $$

15  Map p88, A5

Although just outside Little India, Shish Mahal channels the flavours of northern India and Nepal like few others. From the delicate *momo* (chicken or vegetable-filled dumplings spiked with coriander) to the the slightly smoky, cardamom-spiked *mahal ka makhanwala* chicken, dishes are lively, complex, but never overbearing. Add genuine, friendly service and it's little wonder this place comes up trumps. (www.shishmahal.com.sg; 01-20 Albert Court Hotel & Mall, 180 Albert St; mains $7-18; ⏰11.30am-11.30pm; Ⓜ Little India; 🐾)

Zam Zam

MALAY $

16 Map p88, D6

Mention 'Zam Zam' to any verified Singaporean foodie and watch their eyes light up: here since 1908, this unadorned, tout-fronted dive serves up incredibly good *murtabak*. Filled with succulent mutton, beef, chicken or venison, they're perfectly crisp and golden, yet never greasy. Servings are epic, so it's best to opt for one between two if you're not especially hungry. (699 North Bridge Rd; dishes $4-22; ⏰8am-11pm; Ⓜ Bugis).

STEVE RAYMER/NATIONAL GEOGRAPHIC SOCIETY/CORBIS ©

An open-air stall in Little India

Café Le Caire

MIDDLE EASTERN $$

17 Map p88, E7

Famed for its fortifying Turkish coffee and real-deal Middle Eastern fare, this hole-in-the-wall cafe is an Arab St must. Join lounging *shisha*-smokers and eager diners for salubrious bites like creamy hummus, olives, felafel, pita, salads and succulent kebabs, served as mains or side-dish snacks. To soak up the vibe at its best, head in on a weekend evening. (www.cafelecaire.com; 33 Arab St; ◷10am-3.30am; Ⓜ Bugis; ⏧⫟)

Tekka Centre

HAWKER CENTRE $

18 Map p88, A5

Queue up for biryani, mutton curries, *roti prata* (fried flat bread served with a curry sauce) and *teh tarik* (pulled tea) at Little India's most famous hawker hang-out, Tekka Centre. Foodies flock to the legendary **Ah-Rahman Royal Prata** (stall 01-248; murtabak $4-5; ◷7am-10pm), with *murtabak* so incredibly good, even Singapore's president is a fan – if you're undecided, go for the chicken *murtabak* with cheese. (cnr Serangoon & Buffalo Rds; dishes $3-5; ◷7am-11pm; Ⓜ Little India; ⏧)

Moghul Sweet Shop DESSERT $

19 🍴 Map p88, B5

If you're after a subcontinental sugar rush, tiny Moghul is the place to get it. Sink your teeth into luscious *gulab jamun* (syrup-soaked fried dough balls), harder-to-find *rasmalai* (paneer cheese soaked in cardamom-infused clotted cream) and *barfi* (condensed milk and sugar slice) in flavours including pistachio, chocolate...and carrot. (48 Serangoon Rd; sweets from $1; ⏰11am-11pm; Ⓜ Little India)

Drinking

Maison Ikkoku CAFE, BAR

20 🍺 Map p88, E6

Pimped with Chesterfield banquettes and suspended wooden dressers, Maison Ikkoku keeps coffee geeks purring with speciality brews like syphon, pourover and old-school espresso. Edibles include decent sandwiches, salads, cakes and *musubi*, a sushi-like Hawaiian snack topped with seasoned spam. Two floors up is the slinky cocktail bar, complete with alfresco terrace and a view of Sultan Mosque's golden dome. (www.maison-ikkoku.net; 20 Kandahar St; ⏰cafe 9am-9pm Mon-Thu, to 11pm Fri & Sat, to 7pm Sun, bar 6pm-late Mon-Sat; Ⓜ Bugis; 📶)

Local Life
Sawasdee, Singapore!

If you fancy a quick Thai side trip, make a bee line for seedy, retro **Golden Mile Complex** (Map p88, E6; 5001 Beach Rd; ⏰10am-10pm; Ⓜ Lavender, Bugis). It's Siam in a shopping centre, packed with Thai shops, grocers, butchers and eateries. The Isan (northeast) food is best and ground-floor **Nong Khai** (shop 01-74; dishes from $5; ⏰10am-10pm) is cream of the crop. Stuffed with *sôm-tam* (papaya salad) and Singha, kick on upstairs at **Thai Disco** (shop 02-85; ⏰8pm-3am Sun-Fri, to 4am Sat), where vampish pop princesses and heavily hair-gelled boy bands belt out cheesy Thai pop.

BluJaz Café PUB

21 🍺 Map p88, D7

Brightly coloured and eccentrically decorated, this boho hang-out keeps punters happy with its well-priced beers (from $6), live jazz or blues on Friday and Saturday (and the first Monday of the month) and funky upstairs lounge. Best seats in the house, however, line the side alley linking Bali and Haji Lanes. (www.blujaz.net; 11 Bali Lane; ⏰noon-1am Mon-Thu, noon-2am Fri, 4pm-2am Sat; Ⓜ Bugis; 📶)

Divine

BAR

22 Map p88, D7

Looking like it's straight out of 1930s Manhattan, this wine and cocktail lounge is an art deco–inspired extravaganza, adorned with ornate bronze ceilings, grand piano and a 12m-high wine rack. Order a bottle after 6pm and the in-house wine angel 'flies up' to fetch your shiraz (ignore the pulley). Of course, it just wouldn't be New York without jazz, live nightly from 8.15pm. (Parkview Sq lobby, 600 North Bridge Rd; ⊙11am-1am; Ⓜ Bugis)

Prince of Wales

PUB

23 Map p88, B5

Take 10 from Little India's melee at this popular Aussie-style pub, complete with small, palm-fringed beer garden and a mural of Melbourne

landmarks. There's Gippsland Pale on tap, pool tables and sports screens, as well as live music every night from 9pm (from 10pm Friday and Saturday, open-mic from 5pm Sunday). (www.pow.com.sg; 101 Dunlop St; ⊙9am-1am, to 2am Fri & Sat; Ⓜ Little India)

Hoong Woh Tong

TEAHOUSE

24 Map p88, B6

Set on a street speckled with fortune-tellers, this herbal teahouse will fix you up, no matter what your ailment. Erase those boozy nights with an order of cleansing Wong Lo Kat tea or nourish the body with a cup of Five Flower Tea. For something completely out of the ordinary, opt for the *gui ling gao,* a Chinese herbal jelly served with sugar syrup or honey, and reputedly great for the skin. (01-18 The Bencoolen, 180 Bencoolen St; Ⓜ Bugis)

Zsofi Tapas Bar

BAR

25 Map p88, B5

It's all about the rooftop here, a wonderful and highly unusual space for this part of town, and big enough to (nearly) always find a seat on. Drinks are anything but cheap – expect to pay at least $12 for a beer – but every one of them comes with free tapas, which goes some way to softening the blow when you get the bill. (www.tapasbar.com.sg; 68 Dunlop St; ⊙5pm-1am Mon-Thu, to 2am Fri & Sat, to 11pm Sun; Ⓜ Little India)

Local Life

Drink Local

Skip the bars and do what many of the Indian workers do by buying cans of Kingfisher from a corner shop and kicking back with your mates for a drink at one of Little India's pocket-sized parks. Alternatively, settle in at makeshift **Kerbau Rd Beer Garden** (Map p88, A4; Kerbau Rd; ⊙10am-11pm; Ⓜ Little India), packed nightly with punters downing cheap booze (beer from $3) over Bollywood flicks.

Dunlop St, Little India

Countryside Cafe

CAFE

26 Map p88, B5

Complete with a stack of old *National Geographic* magazines, Little India's cutest cafe is run by welcoming owners, has free wi-fi, not to mention well-priced booze (beer from $5, wine $8). Slap bang beside the Inn Crowd youth hostel, it remains busy in the evenings too. A handful of decent, booze-soaking dishes include Goan fish curry. (71 Dunlop St; ◷5pm-3am Mon, 10am-3am Tue-Sun; ⓜLittle India; ⓦ)

Going Om

CAFE, BAR

27 Map p88, D7

Part cafe, part chill-out space. The chilled-out seating area downstairs offers *shisha,* cocktails, coffees, teas and even 'chakra drinks' of seven colours (one for each chakra). Upstairs has a flexible space for yoga, tarot-card readings and group meditation. There's a house magician on Thursday nights, and live-music gigs on Mondays, Wednesdays, Thursdays and Sundays after 8.30pm. (www.going-om. com; 63 Haji Lane; ◷5pm-1am Sun, Mon, Wed & Thu, to 3am Fri & Sat, closed Tue; ⓜBugis)

Entertainment

Bian Cafe

CHINESE OPERA

28 ⚝ Map p88, E6

Fancy your coffee with a side of live opera? If so, head to this petite

PAUL KENNEDY/LONELY PLANET IMAGES ©

Bollywood posters

Kampong Glam cafe between 3pm and 6pm on Thursdays (admission $8) for short bursts of Beijing Opera tunes. Closet opera divas can even have a go themselves. One floor up is the ambitiously named **Singapore Opera Museum** (admission $5; ⏱11am-7pm Tue-Sun), lined with memorabilia from Singapore's Chinese opera scene. (www.singopera.com.sg; 52 Kandahar St; ⏱11am-10pm Tue-Sun; Ⓜ Bugis)

St Gregory Javana Spa SPA

29 ⭐ Map p88, E7

One of three St Gregory facilities in Singapore, all inside top-end hotels, this soothing spa haven offers ayurvedic therapies, as well as traditional Javanese and Chinese massages,

facials and wraps. Located inside the Park Royal; nonguests can also swim in the gorgeous pool (per day $50). (☎6505 5755; www.stgregoryspa.com; Level 3, Park Royal, 7500A Beach Rd; treatments $30-265; ⏱10am-10pm Mon-Fri, 9am-9pm Sat & Sun; Ⓜ Bugis)

Rex Cinemas CINEMA

30 ⭐ Map p86, A5

Where can you catch the Bollywood blockbusters advertised all over Little India? Why at the Rex, of course. This beautifully renovated historic three-screen theatre shows films from around the subcontinent, most subtitled in English. (2 Mackenzie Rd; tickets $10; Ⓜ Little India)

Wild Rice THEATRE

31 ⭐ Map p88, A4

Singapore's sexiest theatre group is based in Kerbau Rd, but organises shows elsewhere in the city (as well as abroad). Productions range from farce to serious politics, and fearlessly wade into issues not commonly on the agenda in Singapore. (☎6292 2695; www.wildrice.com.sg; 3A Kerbau Rd; Ⓜ Little India)

Shopping

Sifr Aromatics GIFTS

32 Map p88, E7

This Zenlike perfume laboratory belongs to third-generation perfume maker Johari Kazura, whose exquisite creations include the heady East (50mL $140), a blend of oud, rose absolute, amber and neroli. Perfumes range from $80 to $300 for 50mL, while vintage perfume bottles range from $60 to $2000. Those after a custom-made fragrance should call a day before their visit. (www.sifr.sg; 42 Arab St; ⏱11am-8.30pm Mon-Sat, to 5pm Sun; Ⓜ Bugis)

Bugis Street Market MARKET

33 🔒 Map p88, C7

What was once Singapore's most infamous sleaze pit – packed with foreign servicemen on R&R, gambling dens and 'sisters' (transvestites) – is now its largest street market, crammed with cheap clothes, shoes, accessories, manicurists, food stalls and, in a nod to its past, a sex shop. One standout is tiny the **Good Old Days** (Shop CSL/D4, Level 2; ⏱noon-10pm), famed for its '70s to '90s vintage frocks, handbags, jewellery, vintage-inspired heels, and retro odds and ends. (www.bugis-street.com; Victoria St; ⏱11am-10pm; Ⓜ Bugis)

Maison Ikkoku FASHION

Wedged between its ground-floor cafe and rooftop cocktail bar (see **20** 🍸 Map p88, E6) is Maison Ikkoku's in-the-know boutique for fashion-literate guys. Raw exposed brickwork lends an appropriately hip vibe for exclusive and lesser-known labels like Japan's details-obsessed Discovered and indie-chic Lad Musician, with accessories including handmade bags from French label Teddyfish and shoes from America's Yuketen. (www.maison-ikkoku. net; 20 Kandahar St; Ⓜ Bugis)

Mustafa Centre DEPARTMENT STORE

34 🔒 Map p88, C3

A Singapore legend, as much cultural rite of passage as shopping experience, Mustafa's narrow aisles and tiny nooks have everything from electronics, clothing, toiletries, tacky clothes (lurid Bollywood shirts always make great presents), cheap DVDs, gold, moneychangers, a supermarket (it's *the* place to stock up on Indian spices and pickles) and – on Sundays – half the population of Singapore. (www. mustafa.com.sg; 145 Syed Alwi Rd; ⏱24hr; Ⓜ Farrer Park)

Q Local Life
NAS

If Little India leaves you longing for more subcontinental culture, the **Nrityalaya Aesthetics Society** (Map p88, B7; 📞6336 6537; www. nas.org.sg; Stamford Arts Centre, 155 Waterloo St; Ⓜ Little India) can help. The organisation runs classes and workshops in traditional Indian arts, including classical dance, music, meditation and yoga. It also hosts the odd performance. The website isn't always updated, so call or drop in.

Local Life
Haji Lane

Fashion fiends in search of fresher, lesser-known labels flock to **Haji Lane** (Map p88, D7), a pastel-hued strip in Kampong Glam lined with hipster-approved, one-off boutiques. **Dulcetfig** (www.dulcetfig. wordpress.com; 41 Haji Lane; ⊘12.30-9pm Mon-Thu, to 10pm Fri & Sat, 1-8pm Sun) drives female fashion bloggers wild with its cool local and foreign frocks and accessories, which include high-end vintage bags and jewellery. Fashion-literate guys should check out minimalist **K.I.N** (51 Haji Lane; ⊘1-8pm Mon-Sat, 3-7pm Sun), where vintage-inspired shirts from Gitman Bros and design-centric bags from Makr sit beside K.I.N's own street-chic, preppy-cool threads and shoes.

Sim Lim Square   ELECTRONICS, MALL

35 🔒 Map p88, B6

A byword for all that is cut-price and geeky, Sim Lim is not for those un-initiated in the world of SIM cards, RAM, motherboards and soundcards. If you know what you're doing, there are real bargains to be had, but the untutored are more likely to be taken for a ride – check the price at three vendors before bargaining hard. If that just isn't you, head in for cheap, seriously cool mobile-phone and tablet covers. (www.simlimsquare.com.sg; 1 Rochor Canal Rd; ⊘11am-8pm; Ⓜ Bugis)

Little Shophouse   HANDICRAFTS

36 🔒 Map p88, E6

In his little workshop-cum-store, craftsman Robert Sng hand-beads riotously colourful Peranakan slippers. Starting at around $300, each pair takes two months to complete, with many admirers simply framing the shoe covers as works of art in them-selves. Beadwork aside, you can also stock up on Peranakan-style tea sets, crockery, vases, handbags and jewel-lery. (43 Bussorah St; ⊘10am-6pm; Ⓜ Bugis)

Indian Classical Music Centre   MUSIC STORE

37 🔒 Map p88, B5

A tiny shop filled with sitars, tabla and all manner of bells both wear-able and shakeable. Buy CDs to play along to, or sign up for music lessons. (☏6291 0187; www.sitar.com.sg; 26 Clive St; ⊘10.30am-6.30pm Mon-Sat, to 4pm Sun; Ⓜ Little India)

Celebration of Arts   HANDICRAFTS, FURNITURE

38 🔒 Map p88, B5

If you feel a home makeover coming on, dive into this treasure trove for beautiful Indian ornaments, statues, lampshades, cushions, bedspreads, furniture and pashmina shawls. Several larger items aren't displayed, so if you're looking for something in particular, ask the friendly owner. (2 Dalhousie Lane; ⊘9am-9.30pm; Ⓜ Little India)

Ganesh ornaments for sale, Little India

Basheer Graphic Books

BOOKSTORE

39 🔒 Map p88, B8

Sex-up your coffee table at this cornucopia of graphic books and magazines. Located inside the Bras Basah Complex (locally dubbed 'Book City'), it has everything from fashion and design tomes to titles on art, architecture and urban planning. The shop also does a brisk mail-order business, so if you're mid-travel and want to have something mailed to you, staff are happy to help. (www.basheergraphic. com; 04-19 Bras Basah Complex; ⊙10am-8pm Mon-Sat, 11am-6.30pm Sun; Ⓜ Bugis)

Straits Records

MUSIC STORE

40 🔒 Map p88, D7

One of the few alternative music stores in Singapore, Straits stocks hip-hop, hardcore and reggae CDs, as well as some old vinyl, T-shirts and books. CDs from local bands start at around $10. (22 Bali Lane; ⊙2-10.30pm Mon-Wed, 2-10pm Thu, 2-11pm Fri, 1.15-11pm Sat, 12.45-9.30pm Sun; Ⓜ Bugis)

KEVIN CLOGSTOUN/LONELY PLANET IMAGES ©

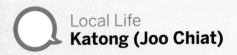

Local Life
Katong (Joo Chiat)

Getting There

M MRT Paya Lebar and Eunos stations are the closest stations.

🚌 Bus Routes 33 and 16 service Joo Chiat Rd.

Also known as Joo Chiat, Katong is the heart of Singapore's Peranakan community. It's an evocative mix of multicoloured shophouses, quaint workshops and handicraft studios, and tucked-away temples, not to mention some of the city's best eateries. Try to head in during business hours, when locals hop in and out of heirloom shops in search of fabrics, produce and the next tasty snack.

❶ Geylang Serai Market

Geylang Serai Market (Geylang Serai) packs in a lively wet market, hawker food centre, and stalls selling everything from Malay CDs to skullcaps. If you're feeling peckish, hunt down some *pisang goreng* (banana fritters) and wash them down with a glass of *bandung* (milk with rose cordial syrup).

❷ Joo Chiat Road

This is one of Singapore's most eclectic streets, lined with dusty antiques workshops, Islamic fashion boutiques and low-fuss grocery shops. Detour left into Joo Chiat Tce to admire the Peranakan terraces at Nos 89 to 129, famed for their carved *pintu pagar* (swinging doors) and colourful ceramic tiles.

❸ Kim's Place Seafood

Back on Joo Chiat Rd, turn left into Joo Chiat Pl. Peer into No 29, a vintage barber, and continue to **Kim's Place Seafood** (www.kims.com.sg; 37 Joo Chiat Pl; mains $4-30; ⏰11am-2.30am) for the city's best claypot black pepper crab.

❹ Kuan Im Tng Temple

Fingers licked, it's a quick walk to **Kuan Im Tng Temple** (www.kuanimtng. org.sg; cnr Tembeling Rd & Joo Chiat Lane), a beautiful Buddhist temple dedicated to Kuan Yin. Temple lovers will appreciate the ornate roof ridges, adorned with dancing dragons.

❺ Koon Seng Road Terraces

Koon Seng Rd is famous for its two rows of prewar, pastel-coloured Peranakan terraces, lavished with stucco dragons, birds, crabs and brilliant glazed tiles imported from Europe. These days they're prized residential real estate, worth around $2.5 million.

❻ Sri Senpaga Vinayagar Temple

One of Singapore's most beautiful Hindu temples, **Sri Senpaga Vinayagar Temple** (19 Ceylon Rd) stuns visitors with its interior of colourful devotional art. One of its star features is the *kamalapaatham,* a specially sculptured granite foot-stone found in certain ancient Hindu temples. The roof of the inner sanctum is covered in gold.

❼ Kim Choo Kueh Chang

Katong is stuffed with bakeries and dessert shops, but **Kim Choo Kueh Chang** (109 East Coast Rd) retains that old-world vibe, selling its traditional pineapple tarts and other brightly coloured Peranakan *kueh* (bite-sized snacks) from a wooden counter that looks more like an apothecary. Upstairs, catch artisans making traditional handicrafts.

❽ Katong Antique House

Tiny shop-cum-museum **Katong Antique House** (☎6345 8544; 208 East Coast Rd) is the domain of Peter Wee. A noted expert on Peranakan culture, Peter will happily regale you with tales as you browse his collection of books, antiques and cultural artefacts. By appointment only, though it's sometimes open to the public.

Local Life
Geylang

Getting There

🚌 **Bus** Routes 2, 13, 21 and 26 run along Sims Ave through Geylang.

Ⓜ **MRT** Aljunied and Paya Lebar are the closest stations.

Contradiction thrives in Geylang, a neighbourhood as famous for its shrines, temples and mosques as for its brothels, sex workers and back-alley gambling dens. Head in for lunch, spend the afternoon wandering quaint *lorongs* (alleys), religious buildings and an under-the-radar gallery, then head back to neon-lit Geylang Rd for a long, lively evening of people-watching and unforgettably good local grub.

❶ Sik Wai Sin Eating House

Geylang is famous for drool-inducing food peddlers, and hot, loud, Cantonese **Sik Wai Sin Eating House** (287 Geylang Rd; 🕑11.45am-2.30pm & 5.45-9.30pm) is living proof. Cult favourites here include homemade tofu fried with giant prawns in egg sauce, pork ribs with bitter gourd and the signature steamed grass carp head in bean sauce.

❷ Amitabha Buddhist Centre

Take a class on dharma and meditation at the seven-floor **Amitabha Buddhist Centre** (📞6745 8547; www.fpmtabc.org; 44, Lorong 25A; 🕑10am-6pm Tue-Sun); its upstairs meditation hall, swathed in red-and-gold cloth, is open to the public and filled with beautiful devotional objects. Check the website for class schedules.

❸ Lorong 24A

One alley worth strolling down is Lorong 24A, lined with renovated shophouses, from which the sounds of chanting emerge – many have been taken over by the numerous small Buddhist associations in the area. Close by, tree-lined Lorong 27 is also worth a wander, jammed with colourful shrines and temples.

❹ Tan Swie Hian Museum

The under-the-radar **Tan Swie Hian Museum** (📞6744 0716; www.tomlinson-collection.com/museum1.html; 460 Sims Ave; 🕑by appointment only Mon-Fri) is dedicated to the work of prolific Singaporean artist Tan Swie Hian, whose works range from vibrant paintings and contemporary sculpture to Chinese calligraphy and poetry.

❺ Sri Sivan Temple

Built on Orchard Rd in the 1850s, the whimsically ornate **Sri Sivan Temple** (www.sstsingapore.com; 24, Geylang East Ave 2; 🕑6am-noon & 6-9pm) was uprooted and moved to Serangoon Rd in the 1980s before moving to its current location in 1993. The Hindu temple is especially unique for its fusion of north and south Indian architectural influences.

❻ Sin Huat Eating House

Roaming food scribe Anthony Bourdain declared **Sin Huat Eating House** (414 Geylang Rd; 🕑11am-late) one of '13 Places To Eat Before You Die'. While it might be expensive, busy and the service brusque, it's hard to fault chef Danny's crab *bee hoon* (rice vermicelli noodles). Ask for prices before committing if you don't want sticker shock later.

❼ Rochor Beancurd

End on a sweet note at **Rochor Beancurd** (745 Geylang Rd; 🕑24hr), a tiny bolthole with an epic reputation. People head here from all over the city for a bowl of its obscenely fresh, silky bean curd (opt for it warm). Order a side of dough sticks and dip to your heart's content. Oh, did we mention the egg tarts?

Local Life
Changi & Pulau Ubin

Getting There

🚌 **Bus** No 2 from Tanah Merah MRT reaches Changi Village. Bumboats (one way $2.50, bicycle surcharge $2; ⏱5.30am-9pm) connect Changi Village to Pulau Ubin.

Singapore's 'Far East' serves up a slower, nostalgic style of local life. Vests, Bermuda shorts and flip-flops is the look in chilled-out Changi Village, where locals are slightly less accustomed to seeing *ang moh* (Westerners) in their midst. A short bumboat (motorised sampan) ride away, the rustic island of Pulau Ubin is the Singapore that development mercifully left behind.

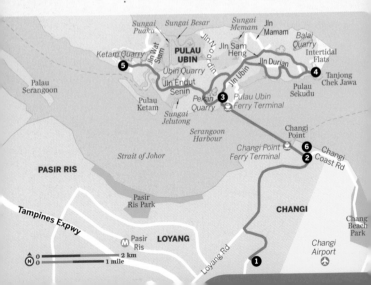

❶ Changi Prison Museum & Chapel

Although no longer at the original Changi prison site, the **Changi Prison Museum & Chapel** (www.changimuseum.com; 1000 Upper Changi Rd North; guided tour adult/child $8/4; ⏰9.30am-5pm) remains a moving tribute to the Allied POWs captured, imprisoned and subjected to horrific treatment by the invading Japanese forces during WWII. Its centrepiece is a replica of the original Changi Chapel built by inmates.

❷ Changi Village

Hugging Singapore's far northeast coast, Changi Village is well worth a wander to experience a curiously relaxed side of Singapore. The vibe is almost villagelike, and a browse around the area will turn up cheap clothes, batik, Indian textiles and electronics. Bumboats to Pulau Ubin depart from Changi Point Ferry Terminal, beside the bus terminal.

❸ Pulau Ubin Village

Your landing spot on Pulau Ubin is Pulau Ubin Village. Although not technically a tourist sight, its ramshackle nature channels a long-lost Singapore. If you're feeling peckish, turn left for a handful of eateries, mostly housed in kampong (village) huts. Tuck into noodles, rice dishes or seafood staples like chilli crab (expect to pay between $20 and $40 for the latter). The village is also the place to rent bikes; day rentals cost around $5 to $10 for adult bikes, and $2 for kids' bikes.

❹ Chek Jawa Wetlands

If you only have time for one part of Pulau Ubin, make it **Chek Jawa Wetlands** (⏰8.30am-6pm). Located at the island's eastern end, its 1km coastal boardwalk juts out into the sea before looping back through protected mangrove swamp to the 20m-high Jejawi Tower, offering a stunning panorama. You can't bring your bike into the reserve so make sure to rent one that comes with a bike lock.

❺ German Girl Shrine

Housed in a yellow hut beside an Assam tree, the German Girl Shrine is one of the island's quirkier sights. Legend has it that the young German daughter of a coffee plantation manager was running away from British troops who had come to arrest her parents during WWI and fell fatally into the quarry behind her house. Somewhere along the way, this daughter of a Roman Catholic family became a Taoist deity, whose help some Chinese believers seek for good health and fortune.

❻ Charlie's Corner

Back in Changi Village, end the day at **Charlie's Corner** (01-08 Changi Village Hawker Centre, 2 Changi Village Rd; dishes from $10; ⏰lunch & dinner Tue-Sun). A veritable institution, its main draws are the endless varieties of beer and the fish and chips.

Explore

Sentosa

Epitomised by its star attraction, Universal Studios, Sentosa is essentially one giant Pleasure Island. The choices are head-spinning, from duelling roller coasters and indoor skydiving to stunt shows and luge racing. Add to this a historic fort, state-of-the-art maritime museum and Ibiza-inspired beachside bars and restaurants, and it's clear why locals head here to live a little.

The Sights in a Day

Only the truly insane would attempt to experience all of Sentosa's attractions in one day, so choose a few and enjoy them thoroughly. You could easily spend the entire day lapping up the rides, shows, food and shops at **Universal Studios** (p112).

Feast on Malay hawker favourites at **Malaysian Food Street** (p117), then spend the afternoon at Universal Studios. Or dabble in history at **Maritime Experiential Museum** (p115), **Images of Singapore** (p115) or **Fort Siloso** (p115). Adrenalin junkie options include indoor skydiving at **iFly** (p118) and luge racing at **Luge & Skyride** (p118), while chill seekers should head to **Underwater World** (p115), **Butterfly Park & Insect Kingdom** (p116) or the luxe **Spa Botanica** (p118).

If you opted for a treatment at Spa Botanica, end the night with sunset mojitos at **Tanjong Beach Club** (p117) and sophisticated supping at **Cliff** (p116). Alternatively, nosh and slosh poolside at **Café del Mar** (p117) before catching the last show at **Songs of the Sea** (p118).

 Top Sights

Universal Studios (p112)

 Best of Singapore

Food & Drink
Cliff (p116)

L'Atelier de Joël Robuchon (p116)

Café del Mar (p117)

For Kids
Universal Studios (p112)

Luge & Skyride (p118)

Songs of the Sea (p118)

Cineblast, 4D Magix & Desperados (p119)

Underwater World (p115)

Butterfly Park & Insect Kingdom (p116)

Escapes
Spa Botanica (p118)

Getting There

Cable car Ride the cable car from Mt Faber or the Harbour-Front Centre.

Monorail The Sentosa Express (7am–midnight) connects Vivo-City to three stations on Sentosa: Waterfront, Imbiah and Beach.

Walk Simply walk across the Sentosa Boardwalk from VivoCity.

Top Sights
Universal Studios

Hankering for a little unadulterated fun? Then Universal Studios is looking at you, kid. The top-draw attraction at Resorts World, its booty of rides, roller coasters, shows, shops and restaurants are neatly packaged into fantasy-world themes based on your favourite Hollywood films. Attractions span the toddler-friendly to the seriously gut-wrenching, spread across a storybook landscape of castles, temples, jungles, retro Americana and sci-fi fantasy. Big kid or small, expect to leave with a blockbuster grin.

Map p114, D2

www.rwsentosa.com

Resorts World Sentosa

adult/child/senior $72/52/36

10am-7pm

Don't Miss

Battlestar Galactica

If you're a hard-core thrill-seeker, strap yourself onto Battlestar Galactica, the world's tallest duelling roller coasters. Choose between the sit-down Human roller coaster or the Cylon, an inverted roller coaster with multiple loops and flips. If you can pull your attention away from screaming, make sure to enjoy the bird's-eye view, not to mention the refreshing breeze.

Revenge of the Mummy

The main attraction of the park's Ancient Egypt section, Revenge of the Mummy will have you twisting, dipping and hopping in darkness on your search for the Book of the Living. Contrary to Hollywood convention, your journey ends with a surprising, fiery twist.

WaterWorld

Gripping stunts, fiery explosions and ridiculously fit eye candy is what you get at WaterWorld, a spectacular live show based on the Kevin Costner flick. Head here at least 20 minutes before show time if you want a decent seat. For a drenching, sit in the soak zone right at the front.

Shrek 4-D

Located in Far, Far Away Castle, Shrek 4-D is one of the top all-ages attractions. Take a seat, slip on your 4-D glasses and join the movie's animated cast on a journey that's bumpy, breezy and just a little bit wet.

☑ Top Tips

▶ Skip entry queues by buying tickets online. Admission is generally cheaper Monday to Friday.

▶ Friday to Sunday is busiest. Avoid public holidays altogether.

▶ On selected Fridays and Saturdays from 7pm to 10pm, Hollywood After Hours allows visitors restricted access to Universal Studios for $5. Purchase tickets at the entrance from 6.30pm.

✗ Take a Break

Cafes and restaurants throughout Universal Studios serve Western and Asian dishes.

For authentic Malaysian hawker food, opt for Malaysian Food Street (p117), an indoor hawker centre just outside the theme-park entrance.

Pulau
Brani

Serapong Golf
Course

Allanbrooke Rd

Tanjong
Golf
Course

Road P

Street 8

Brani Terminal Ave

Selat Sengkir

Bukit Manis Rd

Sentosa Resort

22

6

12

19

Universal Studios

Causeway
Bridge

Sentosa Gateway

Maritime Experiential
Museum

Resorts
World

Gateway Ave

Artillery Ave

Jetty Rd

10

2

9

7

Waterfront

Plaza

Merlion

Imbiah

Beach View

Palawan
Beach

Keppel Harbour

Sentosa Cable Car
station

Images of Singapore

Butterfly Park &
Insect Kingdom

15

Imbiah

4

Beach

14

16

Siloso Rd

Mt Imbiah

20

17

18

8

Siloso
Beach

1

5

Imbiah Walk

Cable Car Rd

11

Underwater
World

21

13

Fort
Siloso

Siloso

3

Seburok Channel

N		
0	500 m	
0	0.25 miles	

Sights

Underwater World
AQUARIUM

1 ⊙ Map p114, B1

Leafy sea dragons and wobbling medusa jellyfish are mesmeric, while stingrays and 3m sharks cruise inches from your face as Underwater World's travelator transports you through the Ocean Colony's submerged glass tubes. If you're game, book a 30-minute **Dive with the Sharks** experience ($120 per person, bookings essential). Entry includes admission to the next-door **Dolphin Lagoon,** where Indo-Pacific humpbacked dolphins perform with seals several times daily (check the show times online). For $170 you can **swim with the dolphins**. Call or book through the Underwater World website. (☑6275 0030; www.underwaterworld.com.sg; behind Siloso Beach; adult/child $25.90/17.60; ⊙10am-7pm)

Maritime Experiential Museum
MUSEUM

2 ⊙ Map p114, C1

The history of the maritime Silk Route gets interactive at this state-of-the-art museum. While the 360-degree Typhoon Theatre is a slight let-down (think 10 minutes of computer-generated wizardry and wind machines), the Maritime Archaeology in Southeast Asia exhibition is genuinely engrossing, with fascinating information on the conservation of shipwreck artefacts. Many of these are on display, including beautiful 15th-century Thai earthenware. The museum gift shop is one of Singapore's best. (www.rwsentosa.com; Resorts World; adult/child museum $5/2, theatre $6/4; ⊙10am-7pm Mon-Thu, to 9pm Fri-Sun, Typhoon Theatre closes 1hr earlier)

Fort Siloso
MUSEUM

3 ⊙ Map p114, A1

This preserved British coastal fort proved famously useless when the Japanese stormed Singapore from the north in WWII. Documentaries, artefacts, animatronics and recreated historical scenes will absorb history buffs, while the underground tunnels are especially fun to explore. (www.sentosa.com.sg; Siloso Point; adult/child $8/5; ⊙10am-6pm, free guided tours 12.40pm & 3.40pm Fri-Sun)

Images of Singapore
MUSEUM

4 ⊙ Map p114, C2

Time travel through seven centuries of Singapore history at this interactive museum, complete with its lifelike wax dummies, film footage and special effects. Despite some inevitable political spin and tacky merchandising, it's genuinely insightful and engaging. (www.sentosa.com.sg; Imbiah Lookout; adult/child $10/7; ⊙9am-7pm)

Butterfly Park & Insect Kingdom

INSECT PARK

5 Map p114, B2

A tropical rainforest in miniature, the Butterfly Park has more than 50 species of butterflies, many of which are endangered and nearly all of which have been bred in the park itself. The Insect Kingdom houses thousands of mounted butterflies, rhino beetles, Hercules beetles (the world's largest) and scorpions. Children stare wide-eyed, while adults feign disinterest. (www.sentosa.com.sg; Imbiah Lookout; adult/child $16/10; ⏱9.30am-7pm)

Top Tip

Entrance Fee & Transport

The entrance fee to Sentosa varies according to the transport chosen: pedestrians walking across from VivoCity pay $1, passengers on the Sentosa Express monorail pay $3, while cable-car passengers have the entrance fee included in the price of the cable car ticket. Once on the island, it's easy to get around, either by walking, taking the Sentosa Express (7am to midnight), riding the free 'beach tram' (shuttling the length of all three beaches, 9am to 11pm, to midnight Friday and Saturday) or by using the three free colour-coded bus routes that link the main attractions (7am to midnight).

Eating

Cliff

SEAFOOD $$$

6 Map p114, D4

Perched high above Palawan Beach (although tree cover obscures some of the view), poolside Cliff serves up sublime seafood to a soundtrack of jazz, crickets and rustling leaves. Expect scallops paired with apples, tuna with watermelon, and barramundi with prosciutto 'floss'. If you're indecisive, opt for the four-course set menu ($130). (www.thecliff.sg; Sentosa Resort, 2 Bukit Manis Rd; mains $58-125; ⏱6.30-10pm)

L'Atelier de Joël Robuchon

INTERNATIONAL $$$

7 Map p114, C2

Adding weight to Sentosa's improving culinary reputation is this svelte nosh spot from French celebrity chef Joël Robuchon. In an open kitchen, chefs diligently upkeep Robuchon's reputation with dishes like seared pâté de foie gras with candied apricots and almonds, and an obscenely comforting steak tartare with flawless French fries. (✆6577 8888; www.joel-robuchon.net; Hotel Michael, Level 1, 101-103 & 104-105, Resorts World; mains $40-95; ⏱dinner)

Coastes

INTERNATIONAL $$

8 Map p114, B2

Coastes is the best of the Sentosa beach eateries, serving up excellent pizzas, pasta and curries to a relaxed crowd. Grab a rustic table under the pergola, or look louche on the sun loungers. It's not exclusively for the hip, tanned and beautiful, as the thumping music suggests. (www.coastes. com; Siloso Beach; ⏱10am-10pm Mon-Thu, 11am-1am Fri & Sat, 9am-10pm Sun)

Malaysian Food Street HAWKER CENTRE $

9 Map p114, C2

With its faux Malaysian streetscape, this indoor hawker centre feels a bit Disney. Thankfully, there's nothing fake about the food itself, cooked by some of Malaysia's best hawker vendors. Pay homage to Singapore's northern neighbour with classics like fragrant *char kway teow* (stir-fried flat rice noodles with chilli, *belacan*, prawns and cockles) and *yong tau foo* (consommé soup with fried tofu, bitter gourd and vegetables). (www. rwsentosa.com; Resorts World; dishes from $3; ⏱11am-10pm)

Samundar INDIAN $$

10 Map p114, D3

Avoid the air-con inside and grab an outdoor table and a few beers and order up big from the tandoor menu at this beachside beauty. The north Indian bias suggests it's aimed squarely at the legions of Indian tourists on Sentosa. Herbivores can rejoice, with plenty of flesh-free options. (www. samundar.com.sg; 85 Palawan Beach Walk; mains $7.60-16; ⏱10.30am-10pm Mon-Thu, to 11pm Fri-Sun; ⚡)

Drinking

Café del Mar BAR

11 Map p114, B2

Café del Mar evidently objects to the idea of a quiet day at the beach, but at night after the deafened day trippers have crept home, this Ibiza-inspired bar comes into its own. Day beds and pastel pouffes on the sand, a poolside bar, Saturday bikini foam parties, DJs...you get the picture. (40 Siloso Beach Walk; ⏱11am-1am Mon-Thu, 11am-4am Fri, 10am-4am Sat, 10am-1am Sun)

Tanjong Beach Club BAR

12 Map p114, D4

The beautiful people flock here to sip cocktails and stretch out on deck chairs. If you don't fancy swimming at the beach, there's also a pool for a dip. Aside from Sunday daytime, it's remarkably quiet, making it an ideal getaway from the madding Sentosa crowds. (www.tanjongbeachclub.com; Tanjong Beach; ⏱11am-11pm Tue-Fri, 10am-11pm Sat & Sun)

Wave House BAR

13 Map p114, B2

Surfer-friendly beach bar with its own ordinary pool as well as two 'flowriders': wave pools that you can pay to surf in (see p118). You can get beers here for $10. (wavehousesentosa.com; Siloso Beach; ⏱10am-11pm)

Entertainment

Songs of the Sea

SHOW

14 ⭐ Map p114, C3

Set around a replica Malay fishing village, this ambitious show fuses Lloyd Webber–esque theatricality with an awe-inspiring sound, light and laser extravaganza worth a hefty $4 million. Prepare to gasp, swoon and (occasionally) cringe. (admission $10; ⏱shows 7.40pm & 8.40pm daily, additional show 9.40pm Sat)

iFly

THRILL RIDE

15 ⭐ Map p114, C2

Freefall from 12,000ft to 3000ft without leaping out of a plane at this indoor skydiving centre. The price includes an hour's instruction followed by two short skydives in a vertical wind chamber. Check the website for off-peak times, which offer the cheapest rates. (www.iflysingapore. com; Beach Station; adult/child from $69/59; ⏱10am-9pm)

Gogreen Segway

TOUR

16 ⭐ Map p114, C3

A little geeky but unashamedly fun, these two-wheeled transporters will have you zipping around a 10-minute circuit or, if you prefer, exploring the beachfront on a guided trip. Equally futuristic are the electric bikes, yours to hire for $12 an hour. Segway riders must be at least 10 years old. (www. segway-sentosa.com; Beach Station; one

circuit $12, 30-minute guided tour $38; ⏱10am-9.30pm)

Luge & Skyride

THRILL RIDE

17 ⭐ Map p114, C2

Take the skyride chairlift from Siloso Beach to Imbiah Lookout, then hop onto your luge (think go-cart meets toboggan) and race along hairpin bends and bone-shaking straights carved through the forest (helmets provided and mandatory!). (1/2/3/5 rides $12.50/18/22/30; ⏱10am-9.30pm)

Wave House

THRILL RIDE

18 ⭐ Map p114, B2

Specially designed wave pools allowing surf dudes and dudettes to practise their gashes and their cutbacks. The pools are part of a bar-restaurant area, which is one of Siloso's coolest hang-outs for youngsters. (www.wavehousesentosa.com; Siloso Beach; 1/2hr surf session from $35/60; ⏱10am-11pm)

Spa Botanica

SPA

19 ⭐ Map p114, D3

For the ultimate Sentosa treat, book a treatment at this spa wonderland, complete with cascading waterfalls, mud pools and lush, landscaped grounds. The signature treatment is the galaxy steam bath, a 45-minute wallow in medicinal chakra mud in a specially designed steam room. A free shuttle connects the spa to VivoCity, as well as to Paragon Shopping Centre on Orchard Rd. (☎6371 1318;

Professional indoor skydivers 11-year-old Choo Yixuan (left) and 10-year-old Kyra Poh at iFly

www.spabotanica.sg; The Sentosa, 2 Bukit Manis Rd; treatments from $80; ⊙10am-10pm)

Cineblast, 4D Magix & Desperados in 3D
THRILL RIDE

20 Map p114, C2

Three attractions offering slightly different variations on the same theme – virtual-reality thrill rides and interactive shows spanning wild water rapids to Wild West shoot-outs. Prepare to get sprayed. (www.sentosa.com.sg; adult/child single attraction $18/11, 3-in-1 combo $37.90/25.90; ⊙10am-9pm)

MegaZip
THRILL RIDE

21 ⭐ Map p114, B2

A 450m-long, 75m-high zip-line from Imbiah Lookout to a tiny island off Siloso Beach. An electric cart is on hand to shuttle riders up from the beach to the start point, where there is also a small adventure park with a climbing wall ($20) and other activities. (www.megazip.com.sg; Siloso Beach; admission $35; ⊙11am-7pm)

Sentosa Golf Club
GOLF

22 ⭐ Map p114, E4

Golf enthusiasts will drool over this luxe golf club, which features two of Asia's finest championship courses. Book well in advance. (☏6275 0022; www.sentosagolf.com; 27 Bukit Manis Rd; green fees per round $280-450, club rental per set $80, buggy fee per person $25, shoe rental $10)

Explore

Holland Village & Tanglin Village

Chic and moneyed, Holland Village is an expat enclave with enough boutiques, cafes, bars and bistros to while away an afternoon and evening. Even leafier is Tanglin Village, a converted barracks packed with a booty of antiques dealers, gourmet delis, restaurants and languid bars. Upstaging them both is the Botanic Gardens, a wonderland of orchids, jungle and romantic dining.

The Sights in a Day

☀ Beat the heat with an early-morning saunter through the **Botanic Gardens** (p122), keeping cool in the ancient rainforest, circling Swan Lake and dropping in on Vanda Miss Joaquim – Singapore's national flower – at the National Orchid Centre. Appetite piqued, head across to **Jones the Grocer** (p127) for eggs, pastries and killer coffee, then shop-hop Tanglin Village for antiques, art and furniture at stores like **Shang Antique** (p133) and **Pasardina Fine Living** (p133).

☀ Spend the afternoon in trendy, expat enclave Holland Village. Pick up a slice of gourmet pizza at **Da Paolo Gastronomia** (p133) before scouring **Holland Village Shopping Centre** (p133) for arts and craft, and **Antipodean** (p133) for threads from in-the-know Singaporean and Australian designers.

☾ Come evening, head back to the Botanic Gardens for romantic noshing at **Au Jardin Les Amis** (p126) or **Halia** (p127) – just make sure you've booked ahead! Wined and dined, head back to Tanglin Village for boutique brews at **Red Dot Brewhouse** (p132) or faultless cocktails at neighbouring **Tippling Club** (p130).

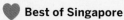

◉ Top Sights

Singapore Botanic Gardens (p122)

♥ Best of Singapore

Eating
Au Jardin Les Amis (p126)
Jones the Grocer (p127)

Drinking
Tippling Club (p130)
Da Paolo Bistro Bar (p131)
Red Dot Brewhouse (p132)

Shopping
Shang Antique (p133)

Getting There

Ⓜ **Metro** Holland Village and the Botanic Gardens both have their own MRT stops on the Yellow Line.

🚍 **Bus** To reach Tanglin Village, catch bus 7, 77, 106, 123 or 174 from behind Orchard MRT, on Orchard Blvd. Bus 7 links Holland Village with Tanglin Village.

Top Sights
Singapore Botanic Gardens

For instant stress relief, take a dose of the Singapore Botanic Gardens. Suddenly the roar of traffic and five million voices melts into the branches, and the world is a tranquil, verdant paradise.
At the tail end of Orchard Rd, Singapore's most famous sprawl of greenery offers more than just picnic-friendly lawns and lakes. It's home to ancient rainforest, themed gardens, rare orchids, free concerts and one of Singapore's most romantic French nosh spots. Breathe in, breathe out.

👁 Map p124, G4

www.sbg.org.sg

Cluny Rd

admission free

🕐 5am-midnight

Ⓜ Botanic Gardens

Swan Lake

Don't Miss

National Orchid Garden

The Botanic Gardens' now famous orchid breeding began in 1928 and you can get the historical low-down at the **National Orchid Garden** (adult/student/child $5/$1/free; ⏲8.30am-7pm). To date, its 3 hectares are home to over 1000 species and 2000 hybrids, around 600 of which are on display – the largest showcase of tropical orchids on Earth.

Rainforest

Older than the Botanic Gardens themselves, this 6-hectare patch of dense primeval rainforest offers a sample of the kind that once carpeted much of Singapore. At the time of writing, a new visitor boardwalk was planned for the area. Of the rainforest's 314 species of vegetation, over half are now considered rare in Singapore.

Ginger Garden

If you thought there was only one type of ginger, the compact Ginger Garden will set you straight. Located next to the National Orchid Garden, this 1-hectare space contains over 250 members of the Zingiberaceae family. It's also where you'll find ginger-centric restaurant Halia (p127). A supporting cast of plants include the little-known Lowiaceae, with their orchidlike flowers.

Swan Lake

For lazy serenity and a touch of romanticism, it's hard to beat Swan Lake (pictured left). One of three lakes in the Botanic Gardens, it's studded by a tiny island cluttered with nibong palms. Look out for the mute swans, imported all the way from Amsterdam.

☑ Top Tips

▶ Excellent, volunteer-run guided tours of the Botanic Gardens take place every Saturday at 9am. Register at the Visitor Centre.

▶ Free classical-music concerts are held regularly in the Botanic Gardens. Check the website for upcoming events.

▶ Buy water when you see it, not when you need it: signage in the Botanic Gardens is not always consistent and backtracking is hardly fun, especially when you're thirsty.

✕ Take a Break

For a chilled, family-friendly vibe and tasty Italian-inspired food, grab a table at Casa Verde (p127).

Those after a more romantic, fine-dining experience shouldn't pass up on lunch or dinner at French hot spot Au Jardin Les Amis (p126).

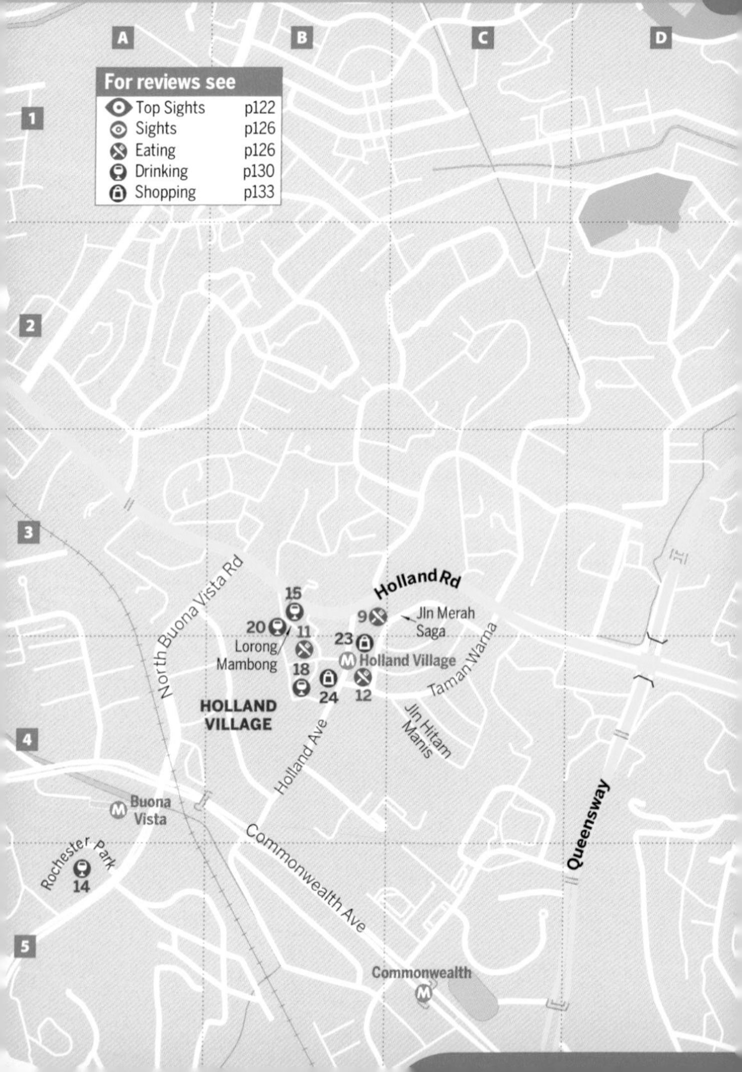

A   B   C   D

1

For reviews see
◉ Top Sights   p122
◎ Sights   p126
✕ Eating   p126
🍷 Drinking   p130
🔒 Shopping   p133

2

3

North Buona Vista Rd

Holland Rd

15

20 11   9 ✕
Lorong   Jln Merah
Mambong   23 🔒 Saga

18   Holland Village

24 12

HOLLAND   Jln Hitam
VILLAGE   Manis

Taman Warna

4

Holland Ave

🅜 Buona
Vista

Rochester Park

14

Commonwealth Ave

Queensway

5

🅜 Commonwealth

E

F

G

H

0 800 m
0 0.4 miles
N

◉1
Memories at
Old Ford
Factory

Bukit Timah Rd

Adam Rd

Dunearn Rd

Rochor Canal

✕8

✕10

Jln
Serene

Cluny Park Rd

Farrer Rd

EW21

Evans Rd

Dalvey Estate

White House Rd

2
✕
5

Cluny Rd

N Nassim Rd

Dalvey Rd

Symphony
Lake

Tyersall Rd

Gallop Rd

Singapore
Botanic
Gardens

Dalvey Gate Rd

Tyersall Ave

✕3

Lermit Rd

Nassim Rd

Singapore
Botanic
Gardens

Nassim Rd

Swan
Lake

Tasman
Serasi

DEMPSEY
HILL

Dempsey Rd

17

Holland Rd

Nassim Hill

Napier Rd

✕4

🔒21

Dempsey Rd

22

Minden Rd

Tanglin
Golf Course

16

Harding Rd

19

✕7 ✕6

13

Loewen Rd

Tanglin Rd

1

2

3

4

5

Sights

Memories at Old Ford Factory

MUSEUM

1 ◎ off Map p124, E1

Site of the humiliating British surrender to the Japanese in 1942, this museum, designed to appeal to young and old alike, tells the story of the Japanese occupation – a watershed period Singapore clearly doesn't want its youth to forget. (www.s1942.org.sg/s1942/moff; 351 Upper Bukit Timah Rd; adult/under 6yr $3/free; ⊙9am-5.30pm Mon-Sat, noon-5.30pm Sun; 🚍170)

Eating

Au Jardin Les Amis

FRENCH $$$

2 ✗ Map p124, G3

If you plan on seducing someone, think romantic colonial-era bungalow, Botanic Gardens backdrop and decadent French fare. Style up, forget the bill and steal a kiss in the gardens afterwards. Daily dinner aside, there's a lunchtime sitting on Fridays (two/three courses $58/70) and a Sunday brunch ($88). Book ahead. (📞6466 8812; www.lesamis.com.sg; EJH Corner House, Singapore Botanic Gardens, Cluny Rd; set dinner menus from $200; ⊙dinner daily, lunch Fri, brunch 11.30am-1.30pm Sun; Ⓜ Botanic Gardens)

MERVIN CHUA / LONELY PLANET IMAGES ©

Jones the Grocer

Halia
FUSION $$$

3 Map p124, G3

With a location like this, nestled amid ginger plants in the Botanic Gardens, who needs good food? Fortunately, Halia provides that as well, with inspired fusion fare like pan-seared and crème brûlée pâté de foie gras, caramelised fig and ice wine jelly. Book a verandah table for a perfect romantic dinner, or savour and save with the good-value set lunch (two/three courses $28/32) Monday to Friday. (☎6476 6711; www.halia.com.sg; Singapore Botanic Gardens, 1 Cluny Rd; mains $40-86; ⏱noon-3pm Mon-Fri, 6.30-10pm Mon-Sat; Ⓜ Botanic Gardens; 🖊)

Samy's Curry Restaurant
INDIAN $

4 Map p124, F5

For over 30 years, the ceiling fans spun above the banana leaves in this leafy, open-walled, timber-shuttered colonial throwback. Alas the timber shutters have gone, but the food remains magnificent and the vibe one of the least pretentious in the neighbourhood. Do not go past the fragrant fishhead curry. (www.samyscurry.com; Civil Service Club, Block 25, Dempsey Rd; mains $6-10; ⏱closed Tue; 🚌7, 77, 106, 123, 174; 🖊)

Casa Verde
INTERNATIONAL $$

5 Map p124, G3

The most accessible and family-friendly restaurant in the Botanic Gardens, 'Green House' serves up

decent Western grub – pasta, salads, sandwiches – plus scrumptious wood-fired pizzas and a smattering of local dishes. Best of all, the alfresco seating area comes with cooling fans for sweat-free noshing. (www.lesamis.com.sg; Singapore Botanic Gardens, 1 Cluny Rd; lunch $9-18, dinner mains $25-30, pizzas $21-25; ⏱7.30am-9.30pm; Ⓜ Botanic Gardens)

Jones the Grocer
CAFE, DELI $$

6 Map p124, E5

Airy, chic, yet fabulously relaxed, posh-nosh grocer Jones is the darling of the expat set. Scan the shelves for gourmet foodstuffs and wine, raid the fromagerie for artisan cheeses, or simply kick back with A-grade coffee, breakfast, salads, sandwiches, tapas or heartier fare like organic beef burgers with Australian Tarago River blue cheese. Head in before 9.30am

Understand
A Political Primer

Politics in Singapore is both everywhere and nowhere.

Everywhere, in the sense that, with the increasingly significant exception of the web pages that pop up on the computer screens of Singapore's citizens, everything you see, read and hear has at some point felt the guiding hand of government. But it's nowhere, in that the ebb and flow of conflicting opinions and ideas in a public forum is almost nonexistent.

Sole Political Force

The People's Action Party (PAP) has held power in Singapore since 1959 and has been virtually the sole political force since 1965, when the island was evicted from the Malay Federation after an uneasy alliance forged in 1963. Prime Minister Lee Kuan Yew famously cried on TV the day Singapore was left to fend for itself, but he's shed few tears since.

The white-clad party he led with steely paternalism is still in control and currently led by his son, Lee Hsien Loong. Opposition voices like JB Jeyaretnam, Francis Seow and Chee Soon Juan have been removed from the political process via lawsuits and financial ruin. (According to Singapore law, bankrupted citizens aren't allowed to run for election.) Many Singaporeans find persuasive the argument that a successful government doesn't need challenging, while others believe that the government – precisely because of its success – ought to be more tolerant of criticism.

Appetite for Change

Yet times may be changing.

In 2006 the ruling PAP won the expected majority in a landslide victory, claiming 82 of the 84 seats in parliament, but their actual votes fell by 8.69%. More than a third of the eligible electorate voted against the incumbent. The appetite for change was even clearer with the election of 2011, which had the highest proportion of contested seats (94.3%) since Singapore achieved its independence in 1965. The election results were telling. The PAP lost a further 6.46% of the electorate, gaining 60.14% of the votes and 81 of the 87 seats. The biggest gains went to the Worker's Party (WP), whose political agenda puts the spotlight on concerns facing the average Singaporean, from the rising cost of housing and transport to the disproportionately high salaries of ministers.

on weekends to avoid the breakfast queues. (www.jonesthegrocer.com; Block 9, Dempsey Rd; breakfast $6.50-20, mains $13.50-28; ⏱9am-11pm Tue-Sun; 🚌7, 75, 77, 106, 123, 174; 🛜)

Barracks Cafe
 INTERNATIONAL $$

Housed in the tall green building called House, cafe-cum-restaurant Barracks Cafe is a decent spot for a bite to eat. Grab a seat on the wood-decked terrace, complete with forest view, and tuck into vibrant, contemporary grub like macadamia-crusted pumpkin salad, grilled prawns with cauliflower couscous or wild truffled mushroom pizza. (www.dempseyhouse.com; 8D Dempsey Rd; mains $22-32, pizza $20-27; ⏱noon-10.30pm Mon-Fri, 11am-10.30pm Sat, 9am-10.30pm Sun; 🚌7, 77, 106, 123, 174)

Miao Yi Vegetarian Restaurant
 VEGETARIAN $$

Even carnivores can expect a little finger licking at this homely gem, hidden away inside a dated suburban mall. Not only are the dishes beautifully presented, they sing with flavour, from the wonderfully textured spicy 'prawn' (crumbed soy with basil leaves, chilli and cashew nuts) to the legendary suckling 'pig', served with a moreish sweet soy sauce. Call ahead on weekends. (📞6467 1331; 03-01/02 Coronation Shopping Plaza, 587 Bukit Timah Rd; dishes $5-15; Ⓜ Botanic Gardens; ✏🛜)

Da Paolo Pizza Bar
 ITALIAN $$

One of three Da Paolo outlets on the street (the fine-dining restaurant is next door and the gourmet deli at No 43) this svelte, bistro-style favourite peddles bubbly, thin-crust pizzas that would make Italy proud. Beyond the dough is a solid choice of salads, salami, cheeses, as well as an Italo-centric wine list. Weekend breakfast options include *piadinas* (flat breads), eggs and pancakes. (www.dapaolo.com.sg; 44 Jln Merah Saga; dishes $16-29; ⏱lunch & dinner Mon-Fri, 9am-10.30pm Sat & Sun; Ⓜ Holland Village; ✏)

Island Creamery
ICE CREAM $

A calorific shrine for many Singaporeans, who don't mind trekking out of their way to this tiny shop for its freshly made ice creams, sorbets and pies. Lick local with regional flavours including *teh tarik* (sweet Indian spiced tea), *kung pao* cashew and the wonderful Tiger beer sorbet, or start an addiction with the apple pie (creamy vanilla ice cream laced with cinnamon, baked apple and bits of biscuit base). (www.islandcreamery.com; 01-03 Serene Centre, 10 Jln Serene; ice cream from $2.80; ⏱11am-10pm Sun-Thu, to 11pm Fri & Sat; Ⓜ Holland Village)

Holland Village Market & Food Centre

HAWKER CENTRE $

11 Map p124, B4

Despite the signboard outside telling foreigners how to navigate hawker centres and describing different dishes, few venture from the pricier

---

Understand
Tanglin Barracks

One of the first constructed in Singapore, Tanglin Barracks made its debut in 1861. The original barrack buildings were spacious, elevated wooden structures topped with thatched *attap* (sugar palm) roofs and able to house 50 men. Among the barracks' amenities were hospital wards, wash houses, kitchens, a library, reading room and school, as well as officers quarters. Extensive renovation between 1934 and 1936 saw the airy verandahs make way for more interior space, though the French-tiled roofs – which had replaced the original thatched ones decades earlier – were thankfully preserved. Home to the British military for over a century, the barracks served as the headquarters of the Ministry of Defence between 1972 and 1989, before their current reinvention as an upmarket hang-out for lattes, cocktails and high-end antiques.

---

restaurants across the road. All the classics are here, from barbecue seafood to Katong laksa to fried *kway teow* (rice noodles). (Lorong Mambong; ⊙10am-late; Ⓜ Holland Village)

Daily Scoop

ICE CREAM $

12 Map p124, B4

Pimped with whimsical murals, Daily Scoop keeps the magic alive with over 40 creative flavours of hand-churned ice cream. Options include brandied figs and honey, strawberry shortcake and ly-chee martini (vodka-infused ice cream), plus milkshakes, waffles and there-goes-the-diet brownies. (www.thedailyscoop. com.sg; 43 Jln Merah Saga; ice cream from $2; ⊙11am-10pm Mon-Thu, to 10.30pm Fri & Sat, 2-10pm Sun; Ⓜ Holland Village)

Drinking

Tippling Club

BAR

13 Ⓟ Map p124, E5

Forest-fringed Tippling Club takes mixology to new heights. Savour the brilliance in cocktails like 'Wake Me Up, F*ck Me Up' (VSOP cognac, fresh espresso and mole bitters) or 'Smoky Old Bastard' (a large whisky served in a glass tube filled with smoke made from dried orange powder and flavoured with maple syrup and banana). Not cheap (cocktails from $21), but worth it. (www.tipplingclub.com; 8D Dempsey Rd; ⊙6pm-late Mon-Fri, noon-3pm & 6pm-late Sat; 🚌 7, 77, 106, 123, 174)

Holland Village Market & Food Centre

Da Paolo Bistro Bar
BAR

14  Map p124, A5

Looking like it's straight off the pages of *Vogue Living,* this tropical-chic gem sits on a lush, secluded street dotted with colonial bungalows. Settle in on the patio and taste-test one of the speciality tea-based cocktails – we love the Oo Lá Lá (oolong ginseng tea-infused gin, Campari, sweet Vermouth and lemon juice). If you can't pull yourself away, contemporary Italian bites and mains will sustain you through the evening. (www.dapaolo. sg; 3 Rochester Park; ⏱bar 5.30-11.30pm Mon-Fri, 2-11.30pm Sat & Sun, restaurant lunch & dinner daily; 🚌74, 91, 92, 95, 191, 196, 198, 200)

Baden
BAR

15  Map p124, B3

The friendliest and most laid-back of the bars in Holland Village, this German bar-restaurant has street-side seating on lively Lorong Mambong, a selection of European beers (from $11) and some decent food ($16 to $36). The pork knuckle with potato and sauerkraut is particularly good. (42 Lorong Mambong; ⏱2pm-1am Mon-Thu, to 2am Fri & Sat, to midnight Sun; Ⓜ Holland Village)

PS Café
CAFE

16  Map p124, F5

Like nearby Jones the Grocer, this is another expat haven on Dempsey, with solid Western food (mains $20 to $30) and scrummy desserts. We like just coming here for a drink, though. Bag a table outside on the terrace, order a freshly ground coffee with a cheeky slice of cake and enjoy the leafy views. (www.pscafe.sg; 28B Harding Rd; ⏰11.30am-5pm & 6.30-10.30pm Mon-Thu, 11.30am-5pm & 6.30pm-1.30am Fri, 9.30am-5pm & 6.30pm-1am Sat, 9.30am-5pm & 6.30-10.30pm Sun; 🚌7, 75, 77, 105, 106, 123, 174)

Red Dot Brewhouse

BAR

17 🍸 Map p124, F4

Tucked away in a quiet part of Dempsey Hill, this microbrewery is Valhalla for beer fiends. Seven brews on tap include a green pilsner, its alien tinge coming from the spirulina used in the brewing process. Food options are generally mediocre, so kick back on the deck and focus on the liquid gold. (www.reddotbrewhouse.com.sg; 25A Dempsey Rd; ⏰noon-midnight Mon-Thu, noon-2am Fri & Sat, 10am-midnight Sun; 🚌7, 77, 106, 123, 174)

🔍 Local Life

Temple Yoga

If the sound of yoga in a Hindu temple makes your chakras glow, **Sri Muneeswaran Hindu Temple** (3 Commonwealth Dr; Ⓜ Commonwealth) should be on your hit list. Believed to be the largest shrine for the deity Sri Muneeswaran in Southeast Asia, it offers free yoga classes on Sundays (4pm to 5pm and 6pm to 7pm) and Mondays (7pm to 8pm).

2am Dessert Bar

BAR

18 🍸 Map p124, B4

Sweet tooths shouldn't miss this chichi dessert bar, where designer treats like basil white chocolate or tiramisu with kahlua jelly and espresso ice cream are given their own wine pairings. The savoury set is not forgotten, with a small yet satisfying list of drinks-friendly edibles including *patatas bravas* (fried slices of potato with garlic mayo) and cheeses. (www.2amdessertbar.com; 21A Lorong Liput; ⏰6pm-2am Mon-Sat; Ⓜ Holland Village)

Hacienda

BAR

19 🍸 Map p124, E5

One of the best bars around the Dempsey Rd area to kick off the shoes in the garden after a long hot day, sink a few mojitos or draught beers under the trees and contemplate the evening sky – at least until the band comes on. (Block 13A, Dempsey Rd; ⏰5pm-midnight Sun-Thu, to 2am Fri & Sat; 🚌7, 77, 106, 123, 174)

Wala Wala Café Bar

BAR

20 🍸 Map p124, B3

Large, raucous but friendly, Wala Wala has been a long-standing favourite with the young expat crowd for its breezy vibe and its live-music bar upstairs. Downstairs it pulls in football fans with its large sports screens. Beers go for $10, a relative bargain in this part of town. (www.imaginings.com.sg; 31 Lorong Mambong; ⏰3pm-1am Sun-Thu, to 2am Fri & Sat); Ⓜ Holland Village)

Shopping

Antipodean
FASHION

Cult Singaporean and Australian labels are the drawcard at this sneaky boutique near Wala Wala (see **20** Map p124, B3), hidden above Harry's Bar. While men are limited to cool tees and jerseys from local outfitter Sundays, women are the winners, with an in-the-know mix of flirtatious, sculptural, distinctive threads from the likes of Al&Alica, Fleur Wood, Rodeo Show and Hansel. Striking heels, creative handbags and artisan jewellery complete the picture. (www.antipodeanshop.com; 27A Lorong Mambong; M Holland Village)

Shang Antique
ANTIQUES, HOUSEWARES

21 Map p124, F5

Specialising in antique religious artefacts from Cambodia, Laos, Thailand, India and Burma, as well as reproductions, there are items in here dating back nearly 2000 years, with price tags to match. Those with more style than savings can pick up beautifully embroidered silk shawls and table runners from $35. Don't be afraid to ask for a 'good price'. (www.shangantique.com.sg; 16 Dempsey Rd; 10.30am-7pm; 7, 77, 106, 123, 174)

Pasardina Fine Living
ANTIQUES, HOUSEWARES

22 Map p124, E5

If you plan on giving your home a tropical Asian makeover, this rambling treasure trove is a good starting point. Inspired by traditional Indonesian design, its collection includes beautiful teak furniture, ceramic and wooden statues, bark lampshades and the odd carved wooden archway. (13 Dempsey Rd; 10am-6pm Mon-Fri, to 7.30pm Sat & Sun; 7, 77, 106, 123, 174)

Da Paolo Gastronomia
FOOD

23 Map p124, B4

This top-notch deli is the perfect place to fuel up for a shopping jaunt around Holland Village. Pick up anything from slices of gourmet pizza to smelly cheeses, crunchy bread or a bottle of vino. Luscious cupcakes, giant meringues and sinfully good tiramisu await those with a wicked inclination. (www.dapaolo.com.sg; 43 Jln Merah Saga; 8am-9pm; M Holland Village)

Holland Village Shopping Centre
MALL

24 Map p124, B4

It might look stuck in 1986, but Holland Village Shopping Centre remains a magnet for expats and fashionable Singaporeans looking for art, handicrafts, homewares and offbeat fashion. Top billing goes to **Lim's Arts & Living** (Shop 01, level 2), packed with carvings, furnishings, stationery and Asian textiles. Shopped out, hit the massage and reflexology peddlers on Level 3. (211 Holland Ave; 10am-8pm; M Holland Village)

Top Sights
Singapore Zoo

Getting There

Singapore Zoo is 22km northwest of the CBD.

Ⓜ **MRT** Catch the North-South (red) line to Ang Mo Kio, then bus 138 to the zoo.

Think zoos are boring or even a little bit cruel? Prepare to eat your words. One of the world's best, Singapore Zoo is a verdant, tropical wonderland of spacious, naturalistic enclosures, freely roaming animals and interactive attractions. Breakfast with orang-utans, dodge flying foxes, mosey up to tree-hugging sloths, even snoop around replica African villages. Then there's the setting: 28 soothing hectares on a lush peninsula jutting out onto the waters of the Upper Seletar Reservoir. Miss it at your own peril.

Orang-utans at Singapore Zoo

Don't Miss

Jungle Breakfast with Wildlife

Orang-utans are the zoo's celebrity residents and you can devour a scrumptious breakfast buffet in their company at **Jungle Breakfast with Wildlife** (Ah Meng Restaurant Terrace; breakfast adult/child $31/20.30; ⏰9-10.30am). If you miss out, get your photo taken with them at the neighbouring Free Ranging Orang-utan Island (11am and 3.30pm) or Free Ranging Orang-utan Boardwalk (4.30pm).

Great Rift Valley of Ethiopia

Featuring cliffs, waterfall and a stream fashioned to look like the Ethiopian hinterland, the evocative Great Rift Valley exhibit is home to Hamadryas baboons, Nubian ibexes, banded mongooses, black-backed jackals and rock hyraxes. You'll also find replica Ethiopian villages, complete with dwelling huts and insight into the area's harsh living conditions.

Boat Cruise

Recharge your batteries on the zoo's relaxing **boat cruise** (⏰9am-5.15pm), which sails along the jungle-fringed Upper Seletar Reservoir. If you're lucky, you might catch sight of a collared kingfisher or a South American stingray. Single trips between Boat Pier 1 (across from White Tiger Habitat) and Boat Pier 2 (beside Rainforest Kidzworld) take 15 minutes.

Rainforest Kidzworld

Let your own little critters go wild at **Rainforest Kidzworld** (⏰8.30am-6pm), a technicolor play area complete with slides, swings, pulling boats and a carousel. Kids can also ride ponies, feed farmyard animals and squeal to their heart's content in the wet-play area. Swimwear is available for purchase on-site if you don't have your own.

---

www.zoo.com.sg

80 Mandai Lake Rd

adult/child $20/13

⏰8.30am-6pm

☑ Top Tips

▶ Consider combining your trip with a visit to the neighbouring Night Safari (p136).

▶ Wear comfortable shoes, a sunhat and sunglasses. Ponchos are available ($5) in case of rain. If you have kids, bring swimwear for Rainforest Kidzworld.

▶ Feeding times are staggered. Check the website for details.

✕ Take a Break

There's no shortage of eateries on-site, serving everything from thin-crust pizza and American fast food to local staples like laksa, Hainanese chicken rice and *nasi lemak* (rice boiled in coconut milk with fried *ikan bilis*, peanuts and a curry dish).

Top Sights
Night Safari

Getting There

Located beside the Singapore Zoo, Night Safari is 22km north-west of the CBD.

M MRT Catch the North-South (red) line to Ang Mo Kio, then bus 138 to the zoo.

Next door to Singapore Zoo, but completely separate, Singapore's acclaimed Night Safari offers a very different type of nightlife. Home to over 120 species of animals, the park's moats and barriers seem to melt away in the darkness, giving you the feeling of travelling through a thrilling jungle filled with the likes of lions, leopards and alligators. The atmosphere is heightened even further by the herds of strolling antelopes, often passing within inches of the trams that take you around.

Night Safari performance

Don't Miss

Electric Tram Tour

Almost everyone heads to the tram queue as they enter, and you should too. These near-silent, open-sided vehicles come with a guide whose commentary is a good introduction to the park's animals and different habitats. The journey lasts for 45 minutes, though we highly recommend that you alight at the designated stops to explore more of the park on foot.

Walking Trails

Get centimetres away from wild spotted felines on the Leopard Trail, and peer at splash-happy cats and the world's largest bat – the Malay flying fox – on the Fishing Cat Trail. The Forest Giant Trial leads you through primeval rainforest, while the outstanding East Lodge Walking Trail awaits with highly endangered babirusas and elegant Malay tigers.

Creatures of the Night

If you have kids in tow, don't miss **Creatures of the Night** (⏱7.30pm, 8.30pm & 9.30pm, plus 10.30pm Fri & Sat), an interactive 30-minute show with stars that include binturongs, civets and an owl. Seating is unassigned, so it's a good idea to arrive a little early to secure a good vantage point. Note that shows may be cancelled in case of wet weather.

www.nightsafari.
com.sg

80 Mandai Lake Rd

adult/child $32/21

⏱7.30pm–midnight

☑ Top Tips

▶ When returning from the safari, you should catch a bus at around 10.45pm as the last MRT train leaves Ang Mo Kio at 11.30pm. Otherwise, expect to pay around $20 for a taxi to the city centre.

▶ Wear comfortable shoes and bring insect repellent and an umbrella, just in case.

✕ Take a Break

Food and drink options abound outside the entrance. **Bongo Burgers** (⏱6pm–midnight) serves tasty burgers. For local specialities there's kampong-inspired **Ulu Ulu** (⏱6–11pm), with both a la carte options and a buffet.

Explore

Southwest Singapore

Home to Singapore's mighty container terminals, this corner of the city is often overlooked by visitors, who pass through only to take the cable car between Mt Faber and Sentosa. But look closer and you'll find some worthy magnets, among them the spectacular Southern Ridges trail, the elegant NUS Museum and nightlife hot spot St James Power Station.

The Sights in a Day

☀ Start with a quick bite-to-go at **VivoCity** (p149). If the **Labrador Secret Tunnels** (p145) have reopened, step inside to experience an eerie wartime relic. Otherwise, check out **Haw Par Villa** (p145) before continuing further on the MRT Yellow Line to Kent Ridge, from where a shuttle bus leads to **NUS Museum** (p144) and its beautiful ancient artefacts and modern art.

☀ Hop back on the MRT and get off at Pasir Panjang for cheap chow at **Eng Lock Koo** (p146). From here, amble up to hilltop **Reflections at Bukit Chandu** (p141) to relive the area's bloody past, then step inside adjoining Kent Ridge Park to begin your easy trek along the jungle-fringed **Southern Ridges** (pictured left; p140) walking trail.

☾ The walk terminates at Mt Faber, where drinks and dinner are served with stunning views at **Jewel Box** (p147). If you can pull yourself away, catch the cable car down to HarbourFront and shake that booty all night long at sexy, infectious **Movida** (p148).

 Top Sights

Southern Ridges (p140)

💗 **Best of Singapore**

Shopping
VivoCity (p149)

For Kids
Southern Ridges (p140)

Entertainment
Movida (p148)

Museums
NUS Museum (p144)

Reflections at Bukit Chandu (p141)

Getting There

Ⓜ **MRT** Southwest Singapore is well served by the MRT. Some attractions have their namesake stations. Otherwise, HarbourFront (Yellow and Purple Lines), Pasir Panjang (Yellow Line), Jurong East (Green and Red Lines) and Kent Ridge (Yellow Line) are useful stations.

Top Sights
Southern Ridges

A series of parks and hills connecting Mt Faber to West Coast Park, the Southern Ridges will have you trekking through the jungle without ever really leaving the city. While the whole route spans 9km, the best stretch is from Kent Ridge Park to Mt Faber. It relatively easy, and serves up some stunning sights, from lofty skyline and jungle vistas to a seriously striking, wavelike walkway.

Map p142, D3

www.nparks.gov.sg

trail admission free

M Pasir Panjang, then 15min walk to Reflections at Bukit Chandu

Dragonfly

Don't Miss

Reflections at Bukit Chandu

Commemorating the last stand of the Malay Regiment against the Japanese in 1942, **Reflections at Bukit Chandu** (www.s1942.org.sg; 31K Pepys Rd; adult/child $2/1; ☺9am-5.30pm Tue-Sun) combines firsthand accounts, personal artefacts and films to describe the brutal battle that almost wiped out the regiment.

Kent Ridge Park

Behind Reflections you'll find Kent Ridge Park. Strangely deserted, you'll have its short yet wonderful canopy walk pretty much to yourself. From here, stroll downhill to **HortPark** (☺7.45am-8pm).

Forest Walk

From HortPark, a leaflike bridge crosses over Alexandra Rd, leading to the stunning Forest Walk. While you can opt for the Earth trail, the Elevated Walkway is more appealing, offering eye-level views of the jungle canopy covering Telok Blangah Hill.

Henderson Waves

Further along you'll hit the remarkable Henderson Waves, an undulating sculptural walkway suspended 36m above the forest floor. The towers that seem to rise straight out of the jungle are part of Reflections at Keppel Bay – a residential development designed by world-renowned architect Daniel Libeskind.

Mt Faber

Stretching 166m above the southern fringe of the city, Mt Faber's terraced trails wind past strategically positioned viewpoints. It's here you'll find the spectacular cable-car service (see p144) to HarbourFront and Sentosa.

☑ Top Tips

▶ The best time to hit the trail is late afternoon. You avoid the worst of the midday heat, and can make it to Mt Faber in time for sunset drinks or dinner.

▶ Wear comfortable shoes, sunglasses and a sunhat. If rain is on the cards, bring an umbrella. And always pack plenty of water.

▶ Bring your camera. The walk delivers beautiful views of the city, jungle and South China Sea.

▶ If you encounter monkeys, do not feed them. This only encourages them to pester humans.

✕ Take a Break

For drinks and high-end dining with stunning island and sea views, head to Jewel Box (p147).

For cheaper, more casual bites, opt for Faber Bistro (p147), also atop Mt Faber.

A Ⓜ Kent Ridge

B

C

D

National University of Singapore

2 ⊚ NUS Museum

Science Park Drive

Portsdown Rd ⊚ 11

Portsdown Ave

Queensway

1

Kent Ridge Park

2

3 ⊚ Haw Par Villa

HortPark

Southern Ridges ⊚

Haw Par Villa Ⓜ

Buona Vista South Rd

3

Pepys Rd

6 ⊚

Ⓜ Pasir Panjang

Pepys Rd

West Coast Hwy

Alexandra Rd

PASIR PANJANG

Labrador Park Ⓜ

Labrador Villa Rd

4

Labrador Secret Tunnels ⊚ 5

Sebarok Channel

4

Labrador Nature Reserve

Port Rd

For reviews see

◈	Top Sights	p140
⊚	Sights	p144
✖	Eating	p146
🍷	Drinking	p147
★	Entertainment	p148
🔒	Shopping	p149

5

E   F   G   H

0   800 m
0   0.4 miles

Singapore River

1

Tiong Bahru Rd

Alexandra Rd

Ⓜ Redhill

Delta Stadium

Tanglin Rd

Henderson Rd

Henderson Park

Lower Delta Rd

Tiong Bahru Park

Ⓜ *Tiong Bahru*

2

Jln Bukit Merah

Ayer Rajah Expwy

Jln Bukit Merah

3

Telok Blangah Hill Park

Southern Ridges

Henderson Rd

Lower Delta Rd

Kampong Bahru Rd

4

✕9

Mt Faber Park ▲ Mt Faber

8 ✕ ◉1

Mt Faber Cable Car

Telok Blangah Ⓜ

✕7

5

Telok Blangah Rd

HarbourFront Ⓜ

13 🔒

⊕12

VivoCity

Sentosa Gateway

Pulau Keppel

Keppel Harbour 10 🚉

Jardine Steps

HarbourFront 🚉

HarbourFront Ferry Terminal

Sights

Mt Faber Cable Car RIDE

 Map p142, G4

Mt Faber is the centrepiece of Mt Faber Park, one of the oldest parks in Singapore. It's also one bookend to the remarkable Southern Ridges walking trail (p140). The most spectacular way to reach the top is on the cable car, which connects Mt Faber to HarbourFront, and to Sentosa beyond it. Note that ticket prices are the same whether you hop on at HarbourFront or Sentosa. A return ticket is only $8 when you make a food/drink purchase at any

Jewel Box; see p147. (www.mountfaber. com.sg; HarbourFront; adult 1-way/return $24/26, child $14/15; ☺8.30am-9.30pm; Ⓜ HarbourFront)

NUS Museum MUSEUM

 Map p142, A1

Located on the campus of the National University of Singapore (NUS), the three small but exquisite galleries here hold some remarkably fine collections. One gallery showcases ancient Chinese ceramics, bronzes and porcelain, another focuses on art from South and Southeast Asia, while a third features the works of Singaporean artist Ng Eng Teng, below.

Understand
The Secret Mural

Dubbed the Grandfather of Singaporean Sculpture, Ng Eng Teng (1934–2001) is well known for his figurative sculptures, which include *The Explorer*, a tribute to the new millennium located outside the Singapore Art Museum (see p32). Known for his fascination with basic geometric forms and their symbolic value, Ng completed part of his formal training at the Nanyang Academy of Fine Arts in Little India in the 1950s. Among his many works at the NUS Museum is a Ciment Fondu mural titled *Tropical Rhapsody* (1972). Commissioned by the Garden Hotel for its hotel lounge, the work slipped into virtual oblivion after hotel renovations in the early 1980s saw a false wall built to cover it. It was only during the dismantling of the artist's larger hotel mural, *Asian Symphony* (1972) – now hanging in the courtyard of the National University Health System building – that a hotel staffer mentioned 'the smaller mural' in the cafe. And so the false wall was removed, *Tropical Rhapsody* was rediscovered, and the NUS Museum's Ng Eng Teng gallery was chosen as its fortunate recipient.

(www.nus.edu.sg/museum; University Cultural Centre, 50 Kent Ridge Cres, National University of Singapore; admission free; ⏱10am-7.30pm Tue-Sat, to 6pm Sunday; M Kent Ridge, then A2 university shuttle bus; 🛜)

Haw Par Villa

MUSEUM

3 ◎ Map p142, A2

For a free freak out, head to this bizarre mythological theme park. Formerly the Tiger Balm Gardens (yes, it's the brainchild of Aw Boon Haw, creator of the medicinal salve Tiger Balm), its psychedelic statues and dioramas capture some rather bizarre scenes from Chinese mythology. Also on-site is the **Hua Song Museum**, an engaging museum offering a glimpse into the lives, enterprises and adventures of Chinese migrants around the world. (262 Pasir Panjang Rd; theme park free, museum adult/child $4/2.50; ⏱9am-7pm, museum to 5pm; M Haw Par Villa)

Labrador Nature Reserve

HISTORICAL PARK

4 ◎ Map p142, D5

Combining historical sites, long trails through a forest area rich in birdlife, great views from Singapore's only sea cliffs and a beachfront park, Labrador Park is well worth an afternoon of your time. Examine the old British guns, hike through the jungle, visit the Secret Tunnels and the pillbox on the beach, then enjoy a picnic nearby. (www.nparks.gov.sg; Labrador Villa Rd; ⏱24hr; M Labrador Park)

Mt Faber cable car

Labrador Secret Tunnels

HISTORICAL SITE

5 ◎ Map p142, D5

A series of storage and armament bunkers built by the British in the 1880s, the Secret Tunnels remained undiscovered for 50 years after WWII. Small, but fascinating, there are displays of artefacts left behind when the British abandoned the tunnels in 1942, as well as the buckled walls from a direct hit from a Japanese bomb. At the time of writing, the tunnels were closed indefinitely for repairs. (www.nparks.gov.sg; Labrador Villa Rd, Labrador Nature Reserve; adult/child $8.60/5.35; ⏱9am-5pm Tue-Sun; M Labrador Park)

Eating

Eng Lock Koo

HAWKER CENTRE **$**

6 Map p142, B3

This small collection of stalls inside a corner-shop premises is perfect for breakfast or lunch if you're on your way to either Reflections at Bukit Chandu or Kent Ridge Park for the Southern Ridges walk. It does tea and coffee, all the usual hawker-centre favourites – chicken rice, *nasi goreng* (fried rice) – and has an airy open-sided seating area. A real locals' favourite. (114 Pasir Panjang Rd; cnr Pepys Rd; mains from $3; ⏱5am-3pm; Ⓜ Pasir Panjang)

Peramakan

PERANAKAN **$$**

7 Map p142, E4

Run by a couple of genial cooking enthusiasts, this paragon of home-style Baba-Nonya cuisine has migrated from its spiritual Joo Chiat home, but the classics such as *sambal* (spicy shrimp paste) squid and *rendang* (spicy coconut curry) remain as good as ever. One dish not to be missed is the *ayam buah keluak* (chicken in a rich spicy sauce served with black, pastelike nut). (www.peramakan.com; L3 Keppel Club, 10 Bukit Chermin Rd; ⏱11.30am-3pm & 6-10pm; Ⓜ Telok Blangah)

St James Power Station (p149)

Jewel Box INTERNATIONAL $$$

8 Map p142, G4

Where the Mt Faber cable car terminates, this smart dining complex serves up a booty of high-end nosh spots, all with fabulous harbour views. Sleek and trendy **Black Opal** (⏱9am-11pm) focuses on Euro flavours, **Sapphire** (⏱11am-11pm Sun-Thu, to 1am Fri & Sat) has an international menu and alfresco seating, while **Empress Jade** (⏱noon-3pm & 6-11pm) serves Chinese cuisine. **Moonstone** (⏱4pm-12.30am Sun-Thu, to 2am Fri & Sat) is the rooftop bar. (⏱6377 9688; www.mountfaber. com.sg; 109 Mt Faber Rd; mains from $25; M HarbourFront)

Sky Dining INTERNATIONAL $$$

Impress the pants off the object of your desires with Sky Dining in the Mt Faber cable car (see 1 ⊙ Map p142, G4) – a romantic three-course dinner with plummeting 60m-high views. Must book online. (⏱6377 9688; www. mountfaber.com.sg; per couple $168-218; ⏱6.30-8.30pm)

Faber Bistro INTERNATIONAL $$

9 Map p142, G4

The most affordable option at the summit of Mt Faber, with a friendly, informal atmosphere, shaded terrace seating and reasonable pastas and salads. On weekends bus 409 runs up here from HarbourFront MRT Station (noon to 9pm). At other times you'll have to take a taxi, ride the cable

Local Life

You've been drinking their beers all holiday, so you might as well see how they're made. Tours of the **Tiger Brewery** (off Map p142; ☏6860 3005; www.apb.com.sg; 459 Jln Ahmad Ibrahim; admission $16; ⏱tours 10am, 11am, 1pm, 2pm, 4pm & 5pm Mon-Fri; M Boon Lay, then ☐182) include a look at the brew house and the packaging hall, plus free beer in the smart Tiger Tavern. Book in advance (online or by phone) and bring photo ID.

car or climb up yourself. It's about 100m up the hill from the Jewel Box. (☏6377 9688; www.mountfaber.com.sg; 101 Mt Faber Rd; mains $13-15; ⏱9am-1am; M HarbourFront)

Drinking

Privé BAR

10 Map p142, E5

Located on an island out in the middle of Keppel Harbour, with the city on one side and Sentosa on the other, you couldn't ask for a better location for evening drinks. Schmooze with an affluent, well-dressed crowd over DJ-spun tunes and the occasional live act. The attached restaurant (mains $25 to $34) serves Euro-American nosh, including succulent steaks, seafood and pasta dishes. (www.prive. com.sg; Keppel Bay Dr; ⏱bar noon-midnight

Sun-Thu, to 1am Fri & Sat, restaurant lunch Mon-Fri, dinner Mon-Sat; HarbourFront, then taxi)

Colbar   BAR, CAFE

11 🚇 Map p142, C1

Something of an institution, Colbar attracts a loyal crowd of weekend regulars drawn to the bare-bones decor, friendly service, wanton Sunday drunkenness and hangover-friendly fry-ups and curries. (9A Whitchurch Rd; ⏱11am-8.30pm Tue-Sun; 🚌100, 123, 147, then walk)

Entertainment

Movida   LIVE MUSIC

12 ⭐ Map p142, H5

Decked out like a '70s disco, this hip-shaking Latin dance club features an excellent, eye-catching, thoroughly danceable band from Paraguay. Of all the venues at St James Power Station, this one's arguably the best. (www.stjamespowerstation.com; St James Power Station, 3 Sentosa Gateway; ⏱8pm-3am Tue-Thu, 8pm-5am Fri & Sat, 6pm-3am Sun; Ⓜ HarbourFront)

Dragonfly   CLUB

Swoon, scream and tear up over pin-ups like *Singapore Idol* contestant Sylvester Sim at this hugely popular mando-pop club near Movida (see 12 ⭐ Map p142, H5), known for its live acts (featuring regulation sexily clad girls and spiky-haired boys), and a curious PVC pipe ceiling design. This is as local as it gets: prepare to be the only foreigner in here. (www.stjamespowerstation.com; St James Power Station, 3 Sentosa Gateway; ⏱6pm-6am; Ⓜ HarbourFront)

Mono   KARAOKE

Wannabe pop stars can belt out their favourite tunes at this swinging karaoke bar (see 12 ⭐ Map p142, H5), done out like a horror-movie French bordello. Facilities include 10 private rooms and a pool table. A couple of bars are on hand to soothe any strained vocal chords. If you need a little Dutch courage, happy hour runs half-price drinks from 6pm to 9pm. (www.stjamespowerstation.com; St James Power Station, 3 Sentosa Gateway; ⏱6pm-6am; Ⓜ HarbourFront)

Top Tip

St James Power Station

It's hard to beat **St James Power Station** (Map p142, H5; www.stjames powerstation.com) for one-stop bars, clubs, and live-music acts. Once a 1920s coal-fired power station, this pumping entertainment complex is home to nine venues, including live-music club Boiler Room, Latin club Movida and Chinese-pop dance club Dragonfly. All the bars and clubs are interconnected, so one cover charge (men $20 Fridays and Saturdays, women free daily) gets you access to all of them. Some bars – Gallery Bar, Lobby Bar and Peppermint Park – have no cover charge at all. Wednesdays' Ladies Night delivers a room-spinning five free drinks to women from 11pm.

Boiler Room   LIVE MUSIC

This straight-up, no-frills rock-and-pop club in St James Powerstation (see 12 🌀 Map p142, H5), is home to top

pop cover band Soul Kool, whose six-nights-a-week extravaganza comes with costume changes and back-up dancers. Wednesday night is hip-hop night, with thumping tunes from across the globe. (www.stjamespowersta tion.com; St James Power Station, 3 Sentosa Gateway; ⏱6pm-3am Mon-Thu, to 4am Fri & Sat; Ⓜ HarbourFront)

Shopping

VivoCity   MALL

13 Map p142, G5

More than just Singapore's biggest shopping mall, waterfront Vivo-City lures locals with its outdoor kids' playground, rooftop 'skypark' (complete with free-to-use paddling pools) and a large Golden Village cineplex. Shopped out and splashed out, retreat to one of its top-notch restaurants and bars, complete with alfresco seating for a soothing sea breeze. (www.vivocity.com.sg; 1 Harbour-Front Walk; Ⓜ HarbourFront)

The Best of
Singapore

Eating in Geylang (p106)
TOM COCKREM/LONELY PLANET IMAGES ©

Best Walks
Colonial Singapore

The Walk

In a city firmly fixed on the future, the Colonial District offers a rare, precious glimpse of a romanticised era and its architectural legacies. This is the Singapore of far-flung missionaries and churches, Palladian-inspired buildings, high-society cricket clubs and the legendary Raffles Hotel. This walk takes in some of the city's most beautiful heritage buildings, swaths of soothing greenery, spectacular skyline views and even a spot of contemporary Asian art. Time it to coincide with a postwalk lunch or dinner by the Singapore River.

Start Singapore Art Museum; Ⓜ Bras Basah

Finish MICA; Ⓜ Clarke Quay

Length 2km; two hours with stops

Take a Break

End your saunter with trademark chilli crab at Jumbo Seafood (p37).

Singapore Art Musem

❶ Singapore Art Museum

The **Singapore Art Museum** (p32) occupies a former Catholic boys school. Original features include the shuttered windows, ceramic floor tiles and inner quadrangle. The central dome and sweeping arcade portico were early-20th-century additions.

❷ Raffles Hotel

Head southeast along Bras Basah Rd, passing the Renaissance-inspired **Cathedral of the Good Shepherd**, and the English Gothic **CHIJMES**, a convent-turned-restaurant complex. Diagonally opposite CHIJMES is the legendary **Raffles Hotel** (p28). Relive its golden era at the Raffles Museum.

❸ St Andrew's

You'll find wedding-cake **St Andrew's Cathedral** further south on North Bridge Rd. Completed in 1838, it was torn down after being struck by lightning (twice!), and rebuilt by Indian convicts in 1862. It's one of Singapore's few surviving examples of English Gothic architecture.

4 **City Hall**

Built in 1928 and featuring a classical facade of Corinthian columns, **City Hall** is where Lord Louis Mountbatten announced Japanese surrender in 1945 and Lee Kuan Yew declared Singapore's independence in 1965. City Hall and the neighbouring Supreme Court, built in 1939, will reopen as the National Art Gallery of Singapore in 2015.

5 **Padang**

Opposite City Hall is the open field of the **Padang**, home to the Singapore Cricket Club and Singapore Recreation Club. It was here that the invading Japanese herded the European community together before marching them off to Changi Prison.

6 **Victoria Theatre**

Below where St Andrew's Rd curves to the left stand a group of colonial-era buildings, including the **Victoria Theatre & Concert Hall**. Completed in 1862, it was originally the Town Hall. It was also one of Singapore's first Victorian Revivalist buildings, inspired by the Italian Renaissance.

7 **MICA**

Hang a right to hit the Singapore River. The multicoloured building on the corner of Hill St is the old Hill St Police Station. Dubbed a 'skyscraper' when built in 1934, it's now known as **MICA** (p35) and is where this journey ends, in true Singaporean style, with old-meets-new rotating exhibitions of contemporary art.

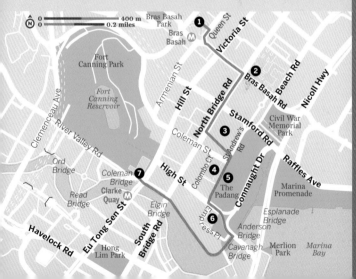

Best Walks
New-Millennium Singapore

The Walk

Singapore is not marching towards the future – it already has one foot in it. Drunk on ambition, the city has been diligently reinventing itself with a bold new wave of quirky, edgy and sometimes controversial developments. This walk will see you exploring the very heart of the 'new Singapore', Marina Bay, a daring precinct where cultural buildings echo fruits and flowers, where bridges recall DNA strings, and where botanic gardens look straight off the set of *The Day of the Triffids*. Welcome to tomorrow.

Start Esplanade – Theatres on the Bay; Ⓜ Esplanade

Finish Marina Bay City Gallery; Ⓜ Bayfront

Length 2km; three hours with stops

Take a Break

End your time travel with a perfect wood-fired crust at Pizzeria Mozza (p37) or gorgeous Gallic dishes at DB Bistro Moderne (p36).

❶ Esplanade – Theatres by the Bay

Singapore's head-turning **Esplanade – Theatres on the Bay** (p43) features a theatre and concert hall under two superstructures of double-glazed laminated glass and aluminium sunshades. Designed by London's Michael Wilford & Partners and Singapore's DP Architects and costing $600 million, it's the world's most expensive sculptural homage to the durian.

❷ Helix Bridge

Walk east along Marina Promenade to the 280m-long **Helix Bridge**. Inaugurated in 2010, it's the world's first double-helix bridge, designed by Australia's Cox Architecture and Singapore's Architects 61. Viewing platforms offer an impressive vantage point for photos across to Collyer Quay, Merlion and Fullerton buildings. At night, LED lighting dramatically shows off the bridge's complex curves.

RACHEL LEWIS/LONELY PLANET IMAGES ©

Helix Bridge

❸ ArtScience Museum

The white, lotuslike building on the other side of the bridge is the **ArtScience Museum**. Opened in 2011, the structure is the work of Israeli-born architect Moshe Safdie, best known for Habitat 76, his 'stack of cubes' residential project in Montreal. Beside it you'll find the world's first floating **Louis Vuitton** store.

❹ Marina Bay Sands

Both the ArtScience Museum and the Louis Vuitton store form part of the ambitious **Marina Bays Sands** integrated resort, home to the lavish **Shoppes at Marina Bay Sands** (p45) and a gravity-defying cantilevered skydeck. Check out the ice-free skating rink, then catch the lift to **Ku Dé Ta** (p39) for a breathtaking vista.

❺ Gardens by the Bay

From Marina Bay Sands, it's an easy walk across to the newly opened **Gardens by the Bay** (p32). Featuring striking space-age conservatories and an aerial walkway, it's the first completed section of what will be a 101-hectare, state-of-the-art botanic garden. It also features 'super-trees' – vertical gardens that look straight out of a 1950s science-fiction film.

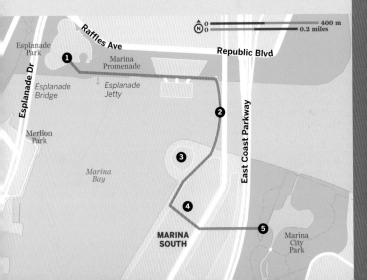

Best
Tours

Best Neighbourhood Tours

Original Singapore Walks
(☎6325 1631; www.singaporewalks.com; adult/child from $30/15) Engaging walking tours, with themes including Chinatown, Little India, Kampong Glam and the Quays. No booking required, simply check the website for meeting places and times.

Real Singapore Tours
(☎6247 7340; www.betelbox.com; tours $80–$100) Insider tours led by Tony Tan and the team at Betel Box hostel. Choose from nature walks, coastline cycling or food odysseys (usually 6pm on Thursday) through the historic Joo Chiat neighbourhood.

Culinary Heritage Tour
(☎6238 8488; www.eastwestplanners.com) Bespoke, top-end tours exploring the city's iconic dishes and where best to eat them. Prices and itineraries available upon request.

Best Water Tours

Singapore River Cruise
(☎6336 6111; www.rivercruise.com.sg; adult/child from $17/13) Jump on a traditional bumboat (motorised sampan) and sail up and down the Singapore River on these 40- and 60-minute tours through the central city.

Imperial Cheng Ho Dinner Cruise
(☎6533 9811; www.watertours.com.sg; adult/child daytime cruise $27/14, dinner cruise $55/29) Three daily tours from Marina South to Sentosa or Kusu Island on a hulking old replica of the Cheng Ho junk. The food may not be spectacular, but the views are.

Singapore Duck Tours
(☎6333 3825; www.ducktours.com.sg; adult/child $33/23) Corny and over-the-top, but shamefully fun – cruise the streets and waterways in a bright, amphibious ex-military vehicle, complete with tinny soundtrack.

DIANA MAYFIELD/LONELY PLANET IMAGES ©

Best Tours with a Twist

Jeffrey Tan
(☎9784 6848; http://jefflimo.tripod.com/jefflimo.htm) 'Singapore's Singing Cabbie' can croon in nine languages and will happily serenade you while showing you the sights of your choice. Tan also offers a food tour, and video karaoke in the limo.

Bukit Brown Tour
(www.bukitbrown.com; admission free) Fascinating walking tours through one of Singapore's most historic, wild and beautiful cemeteries, currently under threat from development. Check the website for upcoming tour dates and times.

Best
Festivals

MICHAEL COYNE/LONELY PLANET IMAGES ©

Hungry Chinese ghosts, fire-walking Hindu faithful, international indie-rock gigs: Singapore's social calendar is intensely eclectic, reflecting both its multicultural make-up and an insatiable determination to shake off its staid, uptight image. It's working, with annual staples including the world's first F1 night race, and Australian indie-music Laneway Festival.

Best Hindu Festivals

Thaipusam (pictured; January) *Kavadis* (heavy metal frames decorated with fruit, flowers and peacock feathers) pierce parading devotees.

Deepavali (October) Little India glows for the 'Festival of Lights'.

Thimithi (November) Hindus walk over white-hot coals at Sri Mariamman Temple.

Best for Musos

Singapore Arts Festival (www.singaporeartsfest.com) World-class music, dance, drama, and art; May/June.

Mosaic Music Festival (www.mosaicmusicfestival.com) Top-notch world-music, jazz and indie acts; May.

Timbre Rock & Roots Festival (www.rockandroots.sg) A-list rock, blues and soul; March/April.

Laneway Festival (http://singapore.lanewayfestival.com.au) Uberhip indie-music fest; February.

Best Chinese Festivals

Chinese New Year (February) Dragon dances, fireworks, food and spectacular street decorations.

Hungry Ghost Festival (August) Fires, food offerings and Chinese opera honour roaming spirits.

Best for Foodies

Singapore Food Festival (www.singaporefoodfestival.com) A month of food stalls, tours, special events and cooking demos; July.

Mooncake Festival (August/September) Lanterns light up Chinatown as revellers feast on mooncakes.

Best Only-in-Singapore Festivals

Chingay (www.chingay.org.sg) Singapore's biggest street party, held on the 22nd day after Chinese New Year; February.

Singapore National Day (www.ndp.org.sg) Patriotic revelry, with extravagant processions, military parades and fireworks. Snap tickets up well in advance; 9 August.

Formula One Night Race (www.f1singapore.com) After-dark F1 racing on a spectacular Marina Bay street circuit; September.

Best
Shopping

Bangkok and Hong Kong might upstage it on the bargain front, but when it comes to choice, few cities match Singapore. Whether you're after Gucci mules, fashion-forward local threads or a 16th-century temple artefact, you'll have little trouble bagging it in Singapore's decadent malls, progressive boutiques and cluttered heirloom businesses. On your marks... Get set... Spend!

Shopping Roadmap

While mall-heavy, fashion-centric Orchard Rd is Singapore's retail queen, it's only one of several retail hubs. For computers and electronics, hit specialist electronics malls like Funan DigitaLife, Sim Lim Square and Mustafa Centre. Good places for antiques include Tanglin Shopping Centre (Map p50, A2), Tanglin Village (p133), and Chinatown (pictured above; p80). For fabrics and textiles, scour Little India and Kampong Glam (p100). Kampong Glam is also famous for its perfume traders, as well as for the booty of hip, independent fashion boutiques on Haji Lane.

Bagging a Bargain

The bad news: prices are usually fixed in all shops, except at markets and some shops in tourist-heavy areas. That said, IT geeks can still look forward to competitive prices and a mind-blowing range of electronics, cameras and gear. While haggling is common at independent electronics stores, especially those inside Sim Lim Square, it should always be good-humoured: don't get petty over a few dollars. Shops in Singapore don't accept returns, though exchanges are accepted if goods have their original tags and packaging.

REX BUTCHER/JAI/CORBIS ©

☑ **Top Tip**

▶ To ensure a good deal on electronics, know the prices back home, and always compare prices at a number of competing businesses.

Best Souvenirs

Little Shophouse (p102) Hand-beaded shoes, ceramics and other Peranakan gifts.

Sifr Aromatics (p100) Bespoke fragrances and vintage perfume bottles.

TWG Tea (p56) Rare, cognoscenti teas from around the world.

Best Malls

ION Orchard (p58) Luxe and High St favourites in a high-tech package.

ION Orchard

Ngee Ann City (p58) Home to Southeast Asia's biggest bookstore.

Paragon (p60) Gloss, glamour and names, names, names, darling.

VivoCity (p149) Singapore's biggest mall, a stone's throw from Sentosa.

313 Somerset (p58) Hip, trendy and hugely popular, with midprice labels and an Apple store.

Best Tech

Funan DigitaLife (p46) Six floors of electronics, cameras and computers.

Sim Lim Square (p102) Bargain-price electronics for seasoned hagglers.

Qisahn (p61) Cut-price video games for gaming geeks.

Best Local Fashion

Front Row (p29) Hip, exclusive labels and accessories from Asia and beyond.

Blackmarket No 2 (p59) Emerging Asian designers and cult French fragrances.

Cathay Cineleisure Orchard (p61) Edgy fashion in a candy-coloured mall.

Mandarin Gallery (p60) Home to retro-inspired, detail-loving Hansel.

Best Fab Finds

Dulcetfig (p102) Quirky local and foreign threads, plus kooky accessories.

Mustafa Centre (p101) No-frills, 24-hour department store peddling just about everything.

Yue Hwa Chinese Products (p81) Five floors of Chinese remedies, foodstuffs, threads, handicrafts and kitsch.

Bugis St Market (p101) Crowds and bargains, from Daisy Dukes to vintage frocks.

Best Art & Antiques

Shang Antique (p133) Original and replica religious artefacts spanning centuries.

Antiques of the Orient (p59) A treasure trove of old Asian books, prints and maps.

Utterly Art (p81) See Singaporean and Filipino art at this private gallery. .

Far East Legend (p80) Pan-Asian objets d'art in a tiny Chinatown shop.

Best
Street Food

It's one of Singapore's great pleasures: ambling into a lively hawker centre in your flip-flops, navigating the steam, smoke and chatter of the stalls, then kicking back with a cold beer and a dirt-cheap feast of mouthwatering regional dishes. And the thrifty feasting doesn't end there, with enough old-school *kopitiams* (coffeeshops) and foodie-approved food courts to keep both tastebuds and wallets purring.

Stalls, Malls & Queues

When it comes to local grub, it's hard to beat Singapore's hawker centres. These large complexes of Chinese, Malay, Indonesian and Indian food stalls are the happiest consequence of the city's cultural stew. They're also great for a cheap feed, with most dishes costing between $3 and $6. If you insist on air-con, head to Singapore's equally famous mall food courts. Unlike their Western counterparts, they peddle fresh, authentic grub for some of the world's pickiest tastebuds. Wherever you go, join the longest queue. While stalls go in and out of favour very quickly, in-the-know Singaporeans are always happy to line up for 30 minutes to savour the very best.

Hawker Centres Decoded

You're at a hawker centre. Now what? Locals always set up base camp before going in search of food. To do this, most place a humble packet of tissues on the table or seat. Table reserved, hit the food stalls. If they bear a 'self-service' sign, you'll have to wait and carry the food back to your table. Other stalls will ask for your table number and deliver the order to you.

Best Hawker Grub

Maxwell Road Hawker Centre (p74) Popular, accessible and famed for its Hainanese chicken rice.

Chinatown Complex (p75) Sprawling labyrinth with legendary dry *bee hoon* (vermicelli noodles).

Tekka Centre (p96) Wriggling produce, saris and city-famous *murtabak* (stuffed savoury pancake).

Nan Hwa Chong Fish-Head Steamboat Corner (p92) Hawker-style vibe and superlative steamboat feasting.

Best Food Courts

Takashimaya Food Village (p54) Basement wonderland of Japanese,

Open-air eating

Korean and other Asian delicacies.

Food Republic (p54) Hawker-style classics and restaurant-style nooks.

Best Snacks

Tong Heng (p75) Veteran pastry shop with sweet and savoury treats from southern China.

Moghul Sweet Shop (p97) Take-away Indian sweets in every colour of the rainbow.

Best Kopitiams

Ya Kun Kaya Toast (p74) Historic hang-out serving Singapore's best runny eggs and *kaya* (coconut jam) toast.

Killiney Kopitiam (p55) Another top spot for old-school Singaporean breakfasts, plus solid curries, laksa and *nasi lemak* (rice boiled in coconut milk, served with fried *ikan bilis,* peanuts and a curry dish).

Best Malay & Indonesian

Warong Nasi Pariaman (p92) Veteran *nasi padang* (Malay rice and the accompanying meat and vegetable dishes) stall with a cultish following.

Zam Zam (p95) Epic, golden *murtabak* in the shadow of a mosque.

Sungei Rd Laksa (p86) A stalwart for fragrant curry broth.

Best Indian

Shish Mahal (p95) Sublime, made-from-scratch north Indian classics.

Bismillah Biryani (p93) Melt-in-your-mouth meats that are famed across Singapore.

Bombay Woodlands (p53) Budget basement brilliance among the Orchard Rd malls.

Best
Dining

Beyond the cheap, wham-bam thrills of hawker centres and food courts is a huge collection of solid restaurants in both the midrange and top-end categories. Options are endless: bolt-hole sushi bars in Orchard Rd malls, halogen-lit Hokkien veterans in Chinatown, trendy tapas bars in Tanjong Pagar, even a haute French hot spot 70 floors above the city. Diet? What diet?

Celebrity Chefs

Ambitious resort developments like Marina Bay Sands have lured an army of celebrity chefs to Singapore, among them Australian prodigy Tetsuya Wakuda and Michelin-starred Daniel Bouland, Joël Robuchon and Mario Batali. So are these hyped hot spots any good? While we confidently recommend those included in this guide, reviews of the city's celeb-chef restaurants are generally mixed, so check locally published food guides and blogs before maxing out your credit card.

Word on the Street

In Singapore, everyone is a food critic and getting consensus between locals on the best places to chomp is tougher than getting agreement on climate change at the UN. Both Singapore *Tatler* magazine's *Best Restaurants* guide and the *Miele Guide* deliver high-end restaurant reviews, while *Time Out* magazine heralds the latest hot spots. Some local food blogs are also insightful: www. ieatishootipost.com, www.bibikgourmand.blogspot. com and www.ladyironchef.com.

☑ Top Tip

▶ Tipping is unnecessary in Singapore, as most restaurants impose a 10% service charge. Tipping at hawker centres will do little more than draw odd looks, so keep your change. Some restaurants don't impose the service charge. In these cases, tip at your discretion.

Best for Romancing

Au Jardin Les Amis
French fine dining in the Botanic Gardens (p126).

Flutes at the Fort (p35) Contemporary Australian nosh in a dreamy colonial bungalow.

Cliff (p116) Stellar seafood and tropical chic in a secluded island setting.

Best Splurge

JAAN (p35) Whimsical French creations 70 floors above the city.

Iggy's (p52) World-renowned East-meets-West twists.

L'Atelier de Joël Robuchon (p116) Near-flawless French from a world-class culinary star.

Best Crab

Jumbo Seafood (p37) Outstanding chilli crab by the river.

Kim's Place Seafood (p105) Can't-be-beaten black pepper crab in Katong.

Best Western & Fusion

DB Bistro Moderne (p36) Gallic gems from celebrity chef Daniel Boulud.

Kilo (p37) Italo-Japanese fusion at an off-the-radar locale.

Esquina (p72) Buzzing tapas bar from UK chef Jason Atherton.

Best Chinese

Royal China (p38) Chinese rarities inside Raffles Hotel.

Din Tai Fung (p53) Smart, respected chain famed for superlative *xiao long bao* (soup dumplings).

My Humble House (p37) Bold, contemporary Cantonese with an artist-designed interior.

Best Peranakan, Indonesian & Indian

Blue Ginger (p72) Still-trendy restaurant with complex Nonya dishes.

Cumi Bali (p72) Indonesian comfort food and a kitschy vibe.

Shish Mahal (p95) Superfresh North Indian and Nepalese nosh.

Best See-&-Be-Seen Breakfast

Jones the Grocer (p127) Posh-nosh deli in an airy colonial conversion.

Wild Honey (p55) Trendy shoppers tucking into all-day breakfasts from around the globe.

Best Cooking Courses

Check booking details and locations of the following courses on the websites.

Cookery Magic (6348 9667; www.cookerymagic.com; classes $65-130) Not only does Ruqxana run standout Asian-cooking classes in her own home, she also conducts them on an ecofarm and in an old kampong home on the bucolic island of Pulau Ubin.

Shermay's Cooking School (6479 8442; www.shermay.com; 03-64 Block 43, Jln Merah Saga, Chip Be Gardens, Holland Village; classes from $90) Singaporean, Peranakan, Thai, chocolate and guest chefs are Shermay's specialities. Hands-on classes are more expensive.

Coriander Leaf (6732 3354; www.corianderleaf.com; 02-03, 3A Merchant Court, Clarke Quay; classes from $120) This Asian fusion restaurant also runs regular classes in Thai, Vietnamese, Italian and French cooking.

Best
for Kids

ANTONY GIBLIN/LONELY PLANET IMAGES ©

Safe, clean, respectable Singapore would make an admirable babysitter. From interactive museum galleries and tactile animal sanctuaries to an island packed with blockbuster theme-park thrills, young ones are rarely an afterthought, with enough activities and exhibitions to thrill kids of all ages and inclinations. Children are welcome almost anywhere... and fawned over enthusiastically. If you're after a little quality family time, Singapore has you covered.

Sentosa: Pleasure Island

While kid-friendly attractions are spread out across Singapore, you'll find the greatest concentration on the island of Sentosa (p110). Here you'll find the LA-style Universal Studios theme park, not to mention a long list of supporting attractions, from Underwater World to Segway tours and decent beaches. You'll need at least a full day to experience everything Sentosa has to offer, not to mention a well-stocked wallet, as most activities, rides and shows cost extra.

Discounts

Kids receive up to 50% discount at most tourist venues. Those under six enjoy free entry to many of Singapore's top museums, including the National Museum of Singapore, Asian Civilisations Museum, and Peranakan Museum. Kids under 90cm tall can ride the MRT for free. Full-time students with photo ID cards also enjoy discounts at many attractions.

☑ **Top Tip**

▶ When visiting Sentosa, be sure to pick up a Sentosa Island map leaflet, available at booths as you enter the island. The map is much larger and more detailed than the one in this guidebook.

Best Museums

National Museum of Singapore (p24) Evocative reconstructions, multimedia displays and child-friendly signage take the boring out of history for kids aged six and up.

Peranakan Museum
(p32) Child-specific activities, audio stories and colourful artefacts keep little ones engaged at this intriguing museum.

Singapore Art Museum
(p32) Top-notch art complete with a children's gallery and periodic kids' activities.

Asian Civilisations Museum (p26) Dress up, play instruments or 'prepare a traditional meal' at the museum's four hands-on Explor-Asian zones.

MINT Museum of Toys
(p35) A jaw-dropping, Technicolor collection of over 50,000 rare, collectable toys from around the globe.

Best Thrills & Spills

Universal Studios
(p112) Hollywood-inspired rides, roller coasters and shows for the young and young-at-heart.

Luge & Skyride (p118) Race the family downhill on a toboggan with wheels.

Singapore Flyer (p34) Reach the skies onboard the world's tallest observation wheel.

Songs of the Sea
(p118) Lights, lasers and a stirring score define this multimillion-dollar spectacular.

Cineblast, 4D Magix & Desperados in 3D
(p119) State-of-the-art movie-watching meets simulated rides.

Best for Health

Southern Ridges (p140) Walk above the jungle and look out for monkeys.

Pulau Ubin (p108) Hop on a bike and cycle through forest and tiny villages on this stuck-in-time island.

Best Eateries

Casa Verde (p127) Family-friendly restaurant in the lush, tropical wonderland of the Botanic Gardens.

Maxwell Road Hawker Centre (p74) Fresh, cheap, no-fuss street

food with a lively, casual vibe.

Daily Scoop (p130) Over 40 dreamy flavours of hand-churned ice cream.

Best Animal Watching

Singapore Zoo (p134) Breakfast with orangutans at one of the world's role-model zoological gardens.

Night Safari (p136) Spend the evening with leopards, lions and Himalayan blue sheep at this atmospheric wildlife oasis.

Underwater World
(p115) Get up close and personal with sharks and surreal sea creatures on an underwater stroll.

Butterfly Park & Insect Kingdom (p116) Coo and wince over beautiful, endangered and dangerous critters.

Best
Drinking

Ditch the kitsch Slings at Raffles. Singapore's slosh spots are a burgeoning scene of rooftop bars, clued-in cocktail dens, Euro-chic wine bars and hipster-pimped coffee roasters. Whatever your poison, you're bound to score: coffee martinis atop CBD and Colonial District skyscrapers, riverside microbrews at Clarke Quay, beachside mojitos on Sentosa, or budget beers on a Chinatown side street.

ANDREW WATSON/ALAMY ©

Cut-Price Drinks

With beers commonly priced between $10 and $18 and cocktails around $20, Singapore is quite possibly the priciest place to sip in Southeast Asia. Save pennies by hitting the bars early for happy-hour specials, usually stretching from 5pm to 8pm and offering discounted libations, cheaper 'housepours' or two drinks for the price of one. If you're not fussed about the decor, join locals at hawker centres or coffeeshops, or hit stalls like Chinatown's Wonderful Food & Beverage (or Little India's Kerbau Rd Beer Garden for cheap cold beer.

Coffee Evolution

While it's no Melbourne or San Francisco, Singapore's speciality coffee revolution is underway. Centred in the hip enclaves of Tanjong Pagar, Tiong Bahru and Kampong Glam is a new wave of clued-in cafes peddling rich, complex coffee made using ethically sourced, locally roasted beans. One of the latest – and best – additions to the scene is Maison Ikkoku, which, aside from offering cognoscenti brewing methods like siphon and pourover, offers rooftop cocktails and a fashion boutique for men.

Best for Beers

Paulaner Bräuhaus German microbrewery with seasonal brews (p40).

Brussels Sprouts Belgian Beer & Mussels Trappist beers and hearty Belgian grub (p40).

Red Dot Brewhouse House-made brews on a languid alfresco deck (p132).

Level 33 Craft beers served with Marina Bay views (p39).

Best for a Tropical Vibe

Café del Mar Ibiza-style beach bar on fun-loving Sentosa (p117) .

Tippling Club Crafty, bespoke cocktails in a jungle-esque setting (p130).

St James Power Station (p149)

Da Paolo Bistro Bar
Chic and discrete, with sleek alfresco lounges, tropical foliage and solid Italian fare (p131).

Best for a View

New Asia Urbane cocktail sessions, 71 floors above the traffic (p38).

1 Altitude Flirt with vertigo at the world's highest alfresco bar (p76).

Lantern Stylish rooftop bar with a dazzling centrepiece pool (p38).

La Terrazza Loud, buzzing crowds atop a film-buff hang-out (p76).

Best for Coffee Snobs

Maison Ikkoku Kampong Glam newbie covering everything from siphon brews and cold pours to old-school espresso (p97).

Plain Creamy lattes, designer mags and a hip, laid-back vibe (p76).

40 Hands Rich espresso and funky murals, slap bang in up-and-coming Tiong Bahru (p83).

Best Local Experiences

Yixing Xuan Teahouse Learn the art of drinking tea (p76).

Wonderful Food & Beverage Cheap, cold beer at a Chinatown street stall (p78).

Café Le Caire People-watch over sucker-punch Turkish coffee and sweetly scented *shisha* (flavoured tobacco smoked in a hookah) (p96).

Kerbau Rd Beer Garden (p98) Bargain booze, Bollywood flicks, and makeshift evening camaraderie.

Best
Entertainment

Once a bespectacled wallflower, Singapore now boasts a full dance card, with more dates than all the Kardashians combined. There are the arts and music festivals, late-night indie gigs, million-dollar megaclubs and Broadway blockbusters, not to mention the home-grown theatre premieres. If you came to Singapore hoping to get bored, bad luck.

Live Music

Music buffs will find a small, kicking local scene, along with world-class music festivals like February's indie showcase Laneway Festival, March's world-music fest Mosaic, and April's Rock and Roots. Esplanade – Theatres on the Bay hosts free concerts, while the Singapore Symphony Orchestra plays free monthly gigs at the Botanic Gardens. A growing number of international pop/rock acts tour Singapore.

Club Culture

Dance clubs proliferate Clarke Quay, while St James Power Station hosts many venues. Serious club kids gravitate to regular international DJ sets at Zouk and Home Club, while Avalon boasts light shows and see-and-be-seen crowds. Zoukout, a beach dance party on Sentosa, is in December. Unless you know someone at the door or get signed in by a member, expect to join queues at the hottest clubs.

The Singapore Stage

Expect quality local and overseas drama at June's Singapore Arts Festival (p157) and regular dance and drama at Esplanade – Theatres on the Bay. Independent theatre groups Singapore Repertory Theatre and Theatreworks deliver new works and international adaptations, while Marina Bay Sands' theatres host visiting Broadway musicals.

☑ **Top Tip**

▶ Check what's on and buy tickets online at www.sistic. com.sg. Expect to pay around $20 to $50 for a ticket to a local theatre production, around $100 to $300 for international music acts, and $65 to $200 for big-budget musicals. Gigs by local music acts at local nightspots are often free.

Best for Live Music

Crazy Elephant (pictured above; p42) A veteran of the scene, with solid rock and blues from local and visiting talent.

Timbre@Substation
(p44) Mostly pop and
indie covers played to an
office-worker crowd.

BluJaz Café (p97) Silky
smooth jazz and blues
in an eclectic Kampong
Glam bar.

Hood (p79) Up-and-
coming venue with
regular performances
from in-demand local
band Timmy.

Home Club (p41) Well
known for showcasing
original local bands.

TAB (p57) A mix of local
and foreign acts playing
anything from acoustic
rock to jazz and comedy.

Movida (p148) Shake
your *culo* (backside)
at this infectious Latin
dance club.

Prince of Wales (p98)
Lively Aussie pub with
garage-style bands
strumming out mostly
acoustic tunes.

Best Clubs

Zouk (p41) Striking
interiors, world-class DJs
and weekly nights span-
ning retro to electronica.

Home Club (p41)
Hip-hop, drum 'n' bass,
techno, deep house,
electro indie...all spun by
globe-trotting A-list DJs.

Zirca Mega Club (p43)
Three clubs in one, play-
ing current dance-floor
fillers, hip-hop and retro.

**St James Power Sta-
tion** (p149) All-in-one entertainment hub spinning
anything from Canto pop
to electro and salsa.

Best for Drama
Queens

**Esplanade – Theatres
on the Bay** (p43) World-
class productions, from
off-Broadway plays to
children's theatre.

**Singapore Repertory
Theatre** (p44) Modern
local works mixed in with
Western classics.

Best LGBT Venues

Tantric (p77) Alfresco
seating, pop diva chart
hits and a flirtatious,
mainly male crowd.

Taboo (p79) Singapore's
main queer dance club,
complete with gym-buff
show-offs and crowded
late-week dance floor.

Backstage Bar (p77)
Laid-back, down-to-
earth Chinatown bar
with friendly service and
a balcony for crowd-
watching.

Best
Views & Vistas

MERTEN SNIJDERS/LONELY PLANET IMAGES ©

Admit it: posting hot travel shots to torture friends is fun. And while it might surprise you, Singapore makes the perfect partner in crime. From dramatic skyline panoramas to close-up shots of brightly coloured shutters, market produce and lurid tropical flora, the city is ridiculously photogenic. So take aim, shoot and relish the envy your pics will incite.

Best Skyline Vistas

New Asia (p38) Spectacular Singapore River panorama; whitewashed colonial buildings northside, CBD towers southside.

Ku Dé Ta (p39) Jaw-dropping views of CBD and Marina Bay skyscrapers, the South China Sea and the sci-fi Gardens by the Bay.

1 Altitude (p76) Skyscrapers so close you can almost touch them.

Best for Architecture Buffs

Ion Orchard Mall (p58) Space-age facade, animated interior panels, retail opulence: commercial architecture at its head-turning best.

Esplanade – Theatres on the Bay (p43) Bold and controversial, Singapore's 'giant durian' delivers countless dramatic angles.

Marina Bay Sands (pictured above; Map p155) A three-tower sci-fi fantasy straight out of *The Jetsons*.

Emerald Hill Rd (p52) An evocative mix of lantern-lit shophouses and elegant, early-20th-century residences.

Best Is-This-Really-Singapore? Backdrops

Little India (p84) Technicolor facades, shrines and garland stalls, mini mountains of spice, and dazzling saris.

Kampong Glam (p84) An 'Arabian Nights' fantasy of late-night *shisha* cafes, intricate Persian rugs and a storybook, golden-domed mosque.

Pulau Ubin (p108) Tin-roof shacks, free-roaming farm animals and rambling jungle wilderness channel a Singapore long since lost.

Geylang Rd, Geylang (p106) An after-dark otherworld of neon-lit karaoke bars, *kopitiams* and seedy side streets of temples and hookers.

Best
for Free

PAUL KENNEDY/LONELY PLANET IMAGES ©

Believe it or not, it is possible to savour some of Singapore's top offerings without reaching for your wallet. Whether you're into ancient artefacts, contemporary art, million-dollar lightshows or live-music gigs, you're bound to find it, free of charge. And then there's the simple pleasure of hitting the city's older, colour-saturated neighbourhoods, where daily life is the best show in town.

Best Always-Free Museums

Baba House (p70) One of Singapore's best-preserved Peranakan dwellings.

NUS Museum (p144) Three well-curated galleries showcasing ancient and modern Asian art and artefacts.

Changi Prison Museum & Chapel (p108) A moving tribute to Singapore's darkest wartime chapter.

Best Sometimes-Free Museums

National Museum of Singapore (p24) Enjoy free entry to the museum's Living History galleries daily from 6pm to 8pm.

Singapore Art Museum (p32) Singapore's top modern-art centre, free between 6pm and 9pm on Friday.

Best Free Art Galleries

Tanjong Pagar Distripark (p73) Established and emerging regional artists in a gallery-packed warehouse.

MICA Building (pictured above; p35) Riverside gallery complex showcasing contemporary Asian talent.

Nanyang Academy of Fine Arts (p90) Interesting rotating exhibitions at one of Singapore's major art schools.

Best Free Entertainment

Esplanade – Theatres on the Bay (p43) Singapore's striking arts hub delivers regular free concerts and events.

Mosaic Music Festival (p157) A 10-day world-music extravaganza, where over half the acts are free to enjoy.

Best Free Only-in-Singapore Experiences

Little India (p84) Soak up the chaos, colour and scents of Singapore's most refreshingly unruly inner neighbourhood.

Chinatown (p62) A visceral jungle of heady temples, medicinal exotica, heritage shop-houses and wriggling market produce.

Best
Museums

Singapore is well endowed with museums, from the tiny and obscure to the ambitious and interactive. You'll find the biggest and the best in the Colonial District, where collections dive into the history, culture and art of Singapore and the continent it belongs to. Beyond them is a kooky booty of unexpected treasures, from reconstructed Chinatown slums to haunting wartime memorials.

FELIX HUG/LONELY PLANET IMAGES ©

Museum Pass Savings

If you're visiting three or more museums during your stay, you can save money by purchasing the 3 Day Museum Pass. Costing $20 (adult) or $50 (for a family of up to five people), the pass offers unlimited admission to eight National Heritage Board museums, including must-sees like the National Museum of Singapore, Asian Civilisations Museum, Singapore Art Museum and Peranakan Museum. Purchase passes at any participating museum; see www.nhb.gov.sg/www/3daymuseumpass.html for a list. Museums in Singapore usually offer significant discounts to full-time students and seniors; bring photo ID.

Lest They Forget

Singapore's WWII experience was a watershed period in its history. You'll see it covered in depth over many museums, including the multimedia-heavy National Museum of Singapore and Images of Singapore. It's also commemorated at several wartime sites, including a British fort on Sentosa, the battleground of Bukit Chandu (Opium Hill) and a former bunker in Fort Canning Park. Not surprisingly, the trauma of occupation and Singapore's tetchy postwar relations with its larger neighbours have fuelled its obsession with security today.

Best Peranakan Pickings

Peranakan Museum (p32) Explore the Peranakan world of marriage, storytelling, fashion and feasting in evocative, multimedia galleries.

Baba House (p70) Step into the private world of a wealthy Peranakan family, c 1928.

Katong Antiques House (p105) A cluttered collection of historical objects and stories from one of Singapore's leading Peranakan historians.

Best for Art & Handicrafts

Asian Civilisations Museum (p26) A Pan-Asian treasure trove of precious decorative arts, religious artefacts, art and textiles.

MERVIN CHUA/LONELY PLANET IMAGES ©

Raffles Museum

NUS Museum (p144) Permanent and temporary exhibitions spanning priceless Chinese ceramics, lesser-known Singaporean history and contemporary Asian art.

Peranakan Museum (p32)

Singapore Art Museum (p32) The world's largest collection of contemporary Southeast Asian art.

Maritime Experiential Museum (p115) Cast your pirate eye over a bounty of shipwreck treasures.

Best for Old Singapore

National Museum of Singapore (p24) Take a multimedia trip through Singapore's tumultuous biography.

Chinatown Heritage Centre (p64) Relive the gritty, chaotic and overcrowded Chinatown of yesteryear.

Images of Singapore (p115) An interactive panorama spanning six centuries of local history.

Raffles Museum (p29) Get nostalgic over maps, posters and celebrity-studded photographs of Raffles Hotel's chic colonial heyday.

Best for War History

Changi Prison Museum & Chapel (p109) Sobering reflections on courage and cruelty during the WWII Japanese occupation.

National Museum of Singapore (p24)

Fort Siloso (pictured left; p115) Slip into subterranean tunnels at this ill-fated defence fort.

Reflections at Bukit Chandu (p141) Get the lowdown on the Japanese invasion at this bite-sized museum atop Opium Hill.

Battle Box (p34) Haunting underground complex documenting the fall of Singapore.

Best
Escapes

GLENN BEANLAND/LONELY PLANET IMAGES ©

Qi blocked? When you have a population density of 7257 people per sq km, it's not surprising. Thankfully, Singapore has myriad ways to revive and refocus weary souls (and soles), from soothing forest canopy walks and island cycling tracks to decadent spa retreats and bargain-priced reflexology joints. Whatever your budget, slow, deep breaths are just around the corner.

City of Parks

Singapore's parks are often masterpieces of design and landscaping, from the renowned Botanic Gardens to the forests of the Southern Ridges. A huge network of park connectors enables cyclists and runners to basically circumnavigate the island without ever encountering a road. For network routes and downloadable maps, see www.nparks.com.sg.

The Rub-Down

Tight muscles have no shortage of salvation, with midrange to luxe spas in most malls and five-star hotels, and a plethora of cheaper no-frills joints in less-fashionable malls like People's Park Plaza. The latter is packed with stalls offering reflexology, shiatsu and even pools of fish that happily nibble away your dead skin cells. Rates vary from around $25 for a foot massage to over $200 for a full-day package.

Best for Pampering

Spa Botanica (p118) Verdant, award-winning indoor/outdoor spa resort on Sentosa.

Willow Stream (p43) Indulgent treatments and luxe facilities at a central city location.

People's Park Complex (p79) The mall might be busy, but the 3rd floor will leave you purring with its cheap reflexology outlets.

Best Green Getaways

Southern Ridges (p140) Thick forest and skyline views dot this string of parks and reserves.

Singapore Botanic Gardens (p122) Catch the MRT to Singapore's manicured paradise.

Pulau Ubin (p108) Cycle your worries away on this quaint, once-upon-a-time island.

Night Safari (p136) For a different kind of nightlife.

Survival Guide

Survival Guide

Before You Go

Book Your Stay

☑ **Top Tip** Midrange and top-end hotel rates are based on supply and demand, with daily fluctuations. During the Formula One night race, for instance, room prices triple.

➡ Singapore is compact, with excellent public transport; your choice of location is not crucial, but it's worth picking carefully. Orchard Rd, best known for large midrange and top-end hotels, is a good choice for shopaholics. Chinatown and Tanjong Pagar are well known for smaller boutique hotels surrounded by atmospheric lanes, restaurants and nightlife. Cheap beds and a backpacker vibe define Little India, while Sentosa delivers resort-

style hotels with easy access to theme parks and beaches.

➡ Book way in advance during peak periods like the Formula One Grand Prix. Even average hostels tend to fill on weekends.

➡ Hostels usually include a simple breakfast. Midrange and top-end hotels usually don't include breakfast unless part of a special deal.

➡ Tipping isn't expected in hostels. It's good form to tip hotel porters and cleaning staff a dollar or two.

Useful Websites

Lonely Planet (www.hotels .lonelyplanet.com) Author-reviewed accommodation and online booking.

Stay in Singapore (www. stayinsingapore.com) User reviews, last-minute deals and online booking.

Agoda (www.agoda.com) Good online deals and booking service.

Trip Advisor (www.trip advisor.com) User reviews and online booking.

Best Budget

Little Red Dot (www.atthe littlereddot.com) Friendly, clean hostel near bustling Little India.

InnCrowd (www.the -inncrowd.com) Wildly popular hostel in the heart of Little India.

Wink Hostel (www. winkhostel.com) Flashpacker newbie with soundproof pods, funky furnishings and Chinatown address.

Best Midrange

Wanderlust (www.wander lusthotel.com) Hip boutique

hotel with creatively themed rooms.

Perak Hotel (www.perak lodge.net) Historic Perana-kan facade and homely rooms in Little India.

Gallery Hotel (www.gall eryhotel.com.sg) Mondrian-inspired facade, cool retro furnishings and glass rooftop pool.

YMCA International House (www.ymcaih.com. sg) Orchard Rd hostel-hotel, with gym, rooftop pool and squash and badminton courts.

Best Top End

Naumi (www.naumihotel. com) Glass and steel bou-tique hotel w ith a petite rooftop infinity pool.

Fullerton Hotel (www. fullertonhotel.com) Five-star elegance in a magnificent colonial building.

Marina Bay Sands (www. marinabaysands.com) Part of the luxury Marina Bay Sands casino complex; jaw-dropping infinity pool.

Capella (www.capellasin gapore.com) Uberluxe rooms, a three-level swimming pool and a lush location on Sentosa.

Arriving in Singapore

☑ **Top Tip** For the best way to get to your accom-modation, see also p17.

Changi Airport

This international **airport** (☎6595 6868, flight informa-tion 1800 542 4422; www. changiairport.com) is about 20km east of the city centre. There are three main terminals and a Budget Terminal.

➡ **Bus** Public bus36 runs from Terminals 1, 2 and 3 to Orchard Rd and the Colonial District ($1.80, one hour). Buses leave roughly every 15 minutes, the first departing at 6.09am and the last just after midnight.

➡ **Airport shuttle** Faster buses (adult/child $9/6, 20 to 40 minutes) leave from all main terminal arrival halls and drop passengers at any hotel, except for those on Sentosa and in Changi Village. They leave from Terminals 1 and 2 and the Budget Terminal (every 15 minutes 6.15pm to midnight, every 30 minutes all other times) and Terminal 3 (every 15

minutes 6am to 10am and 6pm to 2am, every 30 minutes all other times). Booking desks are in the arrival halls.

➡ **MRT** The Mass Rapid Transit offers the best low-cost access into town. The station is below Terminals 2 and 3, the fare to Orchard Rd is adult/child $3/$1.60 (including a $1 refundable deposit). Journey time is around 45 minutes. Change trains at Tanah Merah (just cross the platform). Trains runs between 5.30am and 11.18pm.

➡ **Taxi** Lines at Changi are fast-moving and efficient. The fare structure is com-plicated, but expect to spend anywhere between $18 and $35 into the city centre, depending on the time of travel. The most expensive times are between 5pm and 6am, when numerous surcharges kick in. A limousine transfer service operates 24 hours a day and costs a flat $55 to anywhere on the island.

Train

➡ Trains from Malaysia terminate at **Woodlands Train Checkpoint** (11 Woodlands Crossing; 🚌170,

Causeway Link from Queen St). Three express trains depart daily to Kuala Lumpur (1st/2nd/3rd class $68/34/19), journey time seven to nine hours. Book tickets at the station or online at www.ktmb.com.my.

Bus

➡ Buses arriving from Malaysia drop you either at Lavender St Bus Terminal (Map p88, E2), Queen St Terminal (Map p88, C6) or the Golden Mile Complex (see p97), all of which are in poor locations in terms of late-night transport options.

Calling a taxi is the best option (see opposite).

Boat

There are several main ferry terminals with services from Malaysia and Indonesia.

Changi Point Ferry Terminal (☎6546 85 18; 🚌2, 29, 59, 109) Located 200m north of the bus terminal.

HarbourFront Ferry Terminal (Map p142; ☎6513 2200; www.singaporecruise.com; Ⓜ HarbourFront)

Tanah Merah Ferry Terminal (☎6513 2200; www.singaporecruise.com; 🚌35, then Ⓜ Tanah Merah)

Getting Around

☑ **Top Tip** Singapore is the easiest city in Asia to get around. The *TransitLink Guide* ($2.80 from MRT ticket booths) lists all MRT and bus routes and includes maps showing the surrounding area of all MRT stations. For online bus information, which includes the useful IRIS service (offering live next-bus departure times), see www.sbstransit.com.sg or download the 'SBS Transit Iris' iPhone app. For train information, see www.smrt.com.sg. There's also a consolidated website at www.publictransport.sg.

Mass Rapid Transit (MRT)

➡ Singapore's efficient metro system has four lines: the North-South (Red Line), northeast (Purple Line), East-West (Green Line) and the Circle Line (Yellow Line). Trains run from 5.30am to midnight, running every three minutes during peak times and every four to six minutes off-peak. Single-trip fares cost $1.20 to $2.20 (plus a $1 refundable deposit). If you're planning on

Travel Passes

➡ There are two kinds of pass for Singapore public transport that save a lot of hassle buying tickets every time you travel.

➡ Buy the Ez-link card from the customer service windows at MRT stations for $15, which includes a $5 nonrefundable deposit. It's valid on all buses and trains and will save you up to 30% on fares. The card can be topped up with cash or ATM cards at station ticket machines.

➡ The **Singapore Tourist Pass** (www.thesingaporetouristpass.com) offers unlimited travel on trains and most buses for $8 a day, plus a refundable $10 deposit.

Tourist Buses

Singapore Airlines runs the **SIA Hop-On** (☏9457 2896; www.siahopon.com) tourist bus, traversing the main tourist arteries every 30 minutes daily, starting at Raffles Blvd at 9am, with the last bus leaving at 7.35pm and terminating at Raffles Hotel at 8.55pm. Tickets cost adult/child $12/6, or $6/3 with a Singapore Airlines or Silk Air boarding pass or ticket. Buy tickets from the driver.

City Hippo (☏6338 6877; www.ducktours.com.sg) offers a confusing array of tour options round all the major sites. Twenty-four-hour tickets including a river cruise cost adult/child $33/23.

---

multiple trips, consider purchasing the more convenient Ez-link card or Singapore Tourist Pass.

Bus

➡ Singapore's extensive bus service is clean, extensive and frequent, reaching every corner of the island. The two main operators are **SBS Transit** (☏1800 287 2727; www.sbstransit.com.sg) and **SMRT** (www.smrtbuses.com.sg). Check the websites for information and routes.

➡ Fares range from $1 to $2.10 (less with an Ez-link card). When boarding, drop the exact coins into the fare box (no change is given) or tap your Ez-link card or Tourist Pass on the

reader as you enter and exit the vehicle.

➡ Train operator **SMRT** (www.smrtbuses.com.sg) also runs seven late-night weekend bus services between the city and various suburbs from 11.30pm to 4.30am. See the website for route details.

Taxi

➡ The 'taxi issue' is one of Singapore's big unsolvable problems and finding a taxi at certain times (peak hours, at night or when it's raining) is harder than it should be. The fare structure is complicated, but mercifully metered. Basic flagfall is $3 to $3.40, then $0.22 for every 400m. Some of the many surcharges include 50%

of the metered fare from midnight to 6am, 35% for peak-hour services from 7am to 9am and 5pm to 8pm, $2.30 to $8 for phone bookings and 10% for credit-card payments.

➡ You can flag down a taxi any time, but in the city centre taxis are allowed to stop only at designated taxi stands.

➡ To order a taxi, call **Comfort and CityCab** (☏6552 1111), **Premier Taxis** (☏6363 6888) or **SMRT Taxis** (☏6555 8888).

Essential Information

Business Hours

Exceptions to the following hours are noted in listings.

Shops 10am–6pm; malls and department stores 10am or 11am–10pm

Banks 9.30am–4pm Monday to Friday, some branches close at 6pm, 9.30–11.30am Sat

Restaurants noon–2pm and 6–10pm, casual restaurants, food courts and hawker centres all day

Customs

➡ It is illegal to bring in tobacco unless you pay duty.

➡ The limit on alcohol is 1L of wine, beer or spirits duty-free (and none if you're arriving from Malaysia or Indonesia).

➡ It's illegal to bring in the following items: chewing gum, firecrackers, drugs, pornography, gun-shaped cigarette lighters, endangered species or their by-products, and pirated recordings and publications.

Discounts

➡ If you're arriving on Singapore Airlines or Silk Air, you are entitled to discounts at selected hotels, shops, restaurants and attractions by presenting your boarding pass. See www.singaporeair.com/boardingpass for details.

Electricity

➡ Plugs are of the three-pronged, square-pin type used in the UK. Electricity runs at 230V and 50Hz cycles.

230V/50Hz

Emergencies

Ambulance/Fire (📞995)

Police (📞999)

Holidays

New Year's Day 1 January

Chinese New Year Two days in January/February

Good Friday March/April

Labour Day 1 May

Vesak Day May

National Day 9 August

Hari Raya Puasa October/November

Deepavali October

Christmas Day 25 December

Hari Raya Haji December/January

Money

➡ Singapore's unit of currency is the Singapore dollar.

➡ Cirrus-enabled ATM machines are widely available at all malls.

➡ While banks change money, currency conversion rates are better at the moneychangers dotted all over the city. These tiny stalls can be found in most shopping centres (though not necessarily in the more modern malls). Rates can be haggled a little for amounts over $500.

➡ Credit cards are widely accepted, except at local hawker centres and food courts. Smaller stores may charge an extra 2% to 3% for credit-card payments.

Telephone

➡ There are no area codes within Singapore: telephone numbers are eight digits unless you are calling toll-free (📞1800).

➜ If you plan to use an unlocked phone in Singapore, it's usually cheaper to purchase a local SIM card and number for your mobile. Local SIM cards cost around $18 (including credit) from post offices, convenience stores and local Telco stores; bring your passport.

➜ Roaming charges apply if using your own number, but as Singapore's two cell phone networks (GSM900 and GSM1800) make it compatible with most of the rest of the world you'll still be in business.

➜ In certain areas – mostly along the coast of East Coast Park – Indonesia's signal may push into Singapore's 'airspace', so your calls will be routed through Indonesia – a potentially costly detour!

Useful Phone Numbers

Directory (☎100)

Flight information (☎1800 542 4422)

Singapore international dial code (☎65)

STP Touristline (☎1800 736 2000)

Tourist Information

Singapore Tourism Board (STB; ☎1800 736 2000; www.visitsingapore. com) provides the widest range of services, including tour bookings and event ticketing. There are visitor centres at the following locations: **Bugis Street** (Map p68, C7; 4 New Bugis St; ☉11am-10pm); **Changi Airport** (Terminals 1, 2 & 3; ☉6am-midnight, Terminal 3 to 2am); **ION Orchard** (Map p50, C3; Level 1 Concierge, ION Orchard Mall, 2 Orchard Link; ☉10am-10pm); **Orchard Road** (Map p50; cnr Cairnhill & Orchard Rds; ☉9.30am-10.30pm).

Travellers with Disabilities

➜ Most major hotels, shopping malls and tourist attractions have good wheelchair access, but Little India and Chinatown's crowded narrow footpaths will challenge anyone with mobility, sight or hearing issues. Taxis are usually plentiful, the MRT is wheelchair-friendly and Singaporeans are happy to help out.

➜ The **Disabled Persons Association of Singapore** (www.dpa.org.sg) has information on accessibility in the city.

Visas

➜ Citizens of most countries are granted 30-day entry on arrival by air or overland (though the latter may get 14-day entry). Citizens of India, Myanmar, China, the Commonwealth of Independent States and most Middle Eastern countries must obtain a visa before arriving in Singapore.

Language

The official languages of Singapore are Malay, Mandarin, Tamil and English. Malay is the national language, adopted when Singapore was part of Malaysia, but its use is mostly restricted to the Malay community.

The government's long-standing campaign to promote Mandarin, the main nondialectal Chinese language, has been very successful and increasing numbers of Singaporean Chinese now speak it at home. In this chapter we've provided Pinyin (the official system of writing Mandarin in the Roman alphabet) alongside the Mandarin script.

Tamil is the main Indian language in Singapore; others include Malayalam and Hindi. If you read our pronunciation guides for the Tamil phrases in this chapter as if they were English, you'll be understood. The stressed syllables are indicated with italics.

English is widespread and has been the official first language of instruction in schools since 1987. Travellers will have no trouble getting by with only English in Singapore.

To enhance your trip with a phrasebook, visit **lonelyplanet.com**. Lonely Planet iPhone phrasebooks are available through the Apple App store.

Malay

Hello.	Helo.
Goodbye. (when leaving/staying)	Selamat tinggal./ Selamat jalan.
How are you?	Apa khabar?
Fine, thanks.	Khabar baik.
Please. (when asking/offering)	Tolong./ Silakan.
Thank you.	Terima kasih.
Excuse me.	Maaf.
Sorry.	Minta maaf.
Yes./No.	Ya./Tidak.
What's your name?	Siapa nama kamu?
My name is ...	Nama saya ...
Do you speak English?	Bolehkah anda berbicara Bahasa Inggeris?
I don't understand.	Saya tidak faham.
How much is it?	Berapa harganya?
Can I see the menu?	Minta senarai makanan?
Please bring the bill.	Tolong bawa bil.
Where are the toilets?	Tandas di mana?
Help!	Tolong!

Mandarin

Hello./Goodbye.	你好。/再见。	Nǐhǎo./Zàijiàn.
How are you?	你好吗？	Nǐhǎo ma?
Fine. And you?	好。你呢？	Hǎo. Nǐ ne?
Please ...	请……	Qǐng ...
Thank you.	谢谢你。	Xièxie nǐ.

Excuse me. (to get attention)
劳驾。 Láojià.

Excuse me. (to get past)
借光。 Jièguāng.

Sorry.
对不起。 Duìbùqǐ.

Yes./No.
是。/不是。 Shì./Bùshì.

What's your name?
你叫什么
名字？ Nǐ jiào shénme
míngzi?

My name is ...
我叫…… Wǒ jiào ...

Do you speak English?
你会说
英文吗？ Nǐ huìshuō
Yīngwén ma?

I don't understand.
我不明白。 Wǒ bù míngbái.

How much is it?
多少钱？ Duōshǎo qián?

Can I see the menu?
能不能给我看
一下菜单？ Néng bù néng gěiwǒ
kànyīxià càidān?

Please bring the bill.
请给我账单。 Qǐng gěiwǒ zhàngdān.

Where are the toilets?
厕所在哪儿？ Cèsuǒ zài nǎr?

Help!
救命！ Jiùmìng!

Tamil

Hello.
வணக்கம். va·nak·kam

Goodbye.
போய வருகிறேன். po·i va·ru·ki·reyn

How are you?
நீங்கள் நலமா? neeng·kal na·la·maa

Fine, thanks. And you?
நலம், நன்றி.
நீங்கள்? na·lam nan·dri
neeng·kal

Please.
தயவு செய்து. ta·ya·vu chey·tu

Thank you.
நன்றி. nan·dri

Excuse me.
தயவு செய்து. ta·ya·vu sei·du

Sorry.
மன்னிக்கவும். man·nik·ka·vum

Yes./No.
ஆமாம். /இல்லை. aa·maam/il·lai

What's your name?
உங்கள் பெயர்
என்ன? ung·kal pe·yar
en·na

My name is ...
என் பெயர்... en pe·yar ...

Do you speak English?
நீங்கள் ஆங்கிலம்
பேசுவீர்களா? neeng·kal aang·ki·lam
pey·chu·veer·ka·la

I don't understand.
எனக்கு
விளங்கவில்லை. e·nak·ku
vi·lang·ka·vil·lai

How much is it?
இது என்ன
விலை? i·tu en·na
vi·lai

I'd like the bill/menu, please.
எனக்கு தயவு
செய்து
விலைச்சீட்டு/
உணவுப்பட்டியல்
கொடுங்கள். e·nak·ku ta·ya·vu
chey·tu
vi·laich·cheet·tu/
u·na·vup·pat·ti·yal
ko·tung·kal

Where are the toilets?
கழிவறைகள்
எங்கே? ka·zi·va·rai·kal
eng·key

Help!
உதவி! u·ta·vi

Behind the Scenes

Send Us Your Feedback

We love to hear from travellers – your comments help make our books better. We read every word, and we guarantee that your feedback goes straight to the authors. Visit **lonelyplanet.com/contact** to submit your updates and suggestions.

Note: We may edit, reproduce and incorporate your comments in Lonely Planet products such as guidebooks, websites and digital products, so let us know if you don't want your comments reproduced or your name acknowledged. For a copy of our privacy policy visit lonelyplanet.com/privacy.

Our Readers

Many thanks to the travellers who wrote to us with useful advice and anecdotes:

Bruce Allen, Birgitte Schmidt, Mandy Taylor

Cristian Bonetto's Thanks

A heartfelt *xièxie* to Jasmine Chai, Ally Wong, Eng Teck Cheng, Mark Chng, Wayne Soon and Ian Chong for their generosity and insight. Thanks also to Alvin

Jin Tan, Yu Ying Cheng, Mary-Ann Gardner, Ashleigh Clark, Ryan O'Nell, Toyado Gullem, Brett Bottels and Bubbles.

Acknowledgments

Cover photograph: Marina Bay Sands Singapore and ArtScience Museum; Felix Hug/Lonely Planet Images. Many of the images in this guide are available for licensing from Lonely Planet Images: www.lonelyplanetimages.com.

This Book

This 3rd edition of Lonely Planet's *Pocket Singapore* guidebook was researched and written by Cristian Bonetto. The previous edition was written by Joshua Samuel Brown and Mat Oakley. This book was commissioned in Lonely Planet's Melbourne office, and produced by the following people:

Commissioning Editors Ilaria Walker, Rebecca Currie **Coordinating Editors** Jackey Coyle, Erin Richards **Coordinating Cartographer** James Leversha **Coordinating Layout Designer** Joseph Spanti **Senior Editors** Susan Paterson, Angela Tinson **Managing Editor** Annelies Mertens **Managing Cartographers** Shahara Ahmed, Corey Hutchison **Managing**

Layout Designer Chris Girdler **Assisting Editors** Anne Mulvaney, Charlotte Orr **Cover Research** Naomi Parker **Internal Image Research** Aude Vauconsant **Language Content** Samantha Forge **Thanks to** Sasha Baskett, Laura Crawford, Bruce Evans, Ryan Evans, Larissa Frost, Anna Lorincz, Chris Love, Trent Paton, Kirsten Rawlings, Gerard Walker

Index

See also separate subindexes for:

⊗ **Eating p189**

◐ **Drinking p190**

✪ **Entertainment p190**

🔒 **Shopping p191**

Sights p000
Map Pages **p000**

Sights p000
Map Pages p000

Our Writer

Cristian Bonetto

Cristian's voracious appetite was custom-made for Singapore, and you'll often find him chomping his way across the island in search of culinary enlightenment. Throw in a passion for contemporary architecture, post-colonial politics and retail rampage, and his soft spot for Singapore makes perfect sense. After graduating from the University of Melbourne with a degree in politics and cultural studies, Cristian wrote for both stage and screen before dedicating his life to frequent flyer miles. His musings on food, culture and design have appeared in newspapers and magazines worldwide, as well as online. To date, Cristian's Lonely Planet titles include *New York City*, *Italy*, *Naples & the Amalfi Coast*, *Copenhagen Encounter*, and *Denmark*.

Published by Lonely Planet Publications Pty Ltd
ABN 36 005 607 983
3rd edition – Nov 2012
ISBN 978 1 74220 209 9
© Lonely Planet 2012 Photographs © as indicated 2012
10 9 8 7 6 5 4 3 2 1
Printed in China